# Groovy Programming Language for DevSecOps

Agile Scripting to Secure and Streamline Software
Delivery With Groovy

Davis Simon

# Discover Other Books in the Series

"Groovy Programming Language for Beginners: Your First Steps into Coding"

"Groovy Programming Language for Backend Development:Discover How Groovy Can Revolutionize Your Backend Code"

"Groovy Programming Language for Automation: Unlock the full potential of Groovy to streamline workflows, simplify coding"

"Groovy Programming language for Chatbots:The Ultimate Guide to Building Intelligent Chatbots with Ease"

"Groovy Programming Language for Data Science: Unlock the Power of Seamless Data Analysis and Automation"

"Groovy Programming Language for Web Development: Building Your First Web App"

"Groovy Programming Language for Big Data:Groovy to Build Scalable, Efficient, and Flexible Big Data Applications"

"Groovy Programming Language for Data Manipulation: Master the Basics and Unlock Advanced Techniques for Game-Changing Results"

# Disclaimer

The Book titled " ***Groovy Programming Language for DevSecOps: Agile Scripting to Secure and Streamline Software Delivery*** *With Groovy* " by Davis Simon is intended for educational and informational purposes only.

The content provided in this Book is based on the author's experience, research, and personal opinions. It is designed to offer insights and techniques for backend development using the Groovy programming language.

# Introduction

In the contemporary digital environment characterized by rapid advancements, the integration of development, security, and operations—commonly referred to as DevSecOps—has become vital for organizations aiming to optimize their software delivery processes while maintaining strong security protocols. As companies increasingly depend on swift software development and deployment, the importance of effectively automating and incorporating security within the DevOps lifecycle has reached unprecedented levels.

This is where the Groovy programming language proves invaluable. Known for its ease of use, dynamic characteristics, and excellent compatibility with the Java ecosystem, Groovy emerges as a formidable asset for scripting in DevSecOps settings. Its clear syntax and adaptability enable developers and operations teams to create scripts that automate processes, embed security protocols, and improve the overall efficiency of software delivery.

In "Groovy Programming Language for DevSecOps: Agile Scripting to Secure and Streamline Software Delivery With Groovy," we explore the numerous ways in which Groovy can assist you in fulfilling your DevSecOps goals. This ebook is designed to navigate the complexities of the Groovy language while highlighting its role in securing applications and automating workflows. Whether you are an experienced developer, a DevOps expert, or a security specialist, this book aims to equip you with the insights and skills necessary to utilize Groovy effectively.You'll start by understanding the core principles of Groovy, including its syntax, features, and best practices. From there, we will explore how to leverage Groovy for automating CI/CD pipelines, integrating security testing, and orchestrating infrastructure as code (IaC) workflows. Each chapter is filled with practical examples, code snippets, and real-world scenarios to illustrate how Groovy can simplify complex tasks, reduce manual overhead, and strengthen your security posture.

By the end of this journey, you will not only have a comprehensive understanding of Groovy but also the confidence to implement its capabilities in your DevSecOps practices. Join us as we explore the synergy between Groovy and DevSecOps, paving the way for secure, efficient, and agile software delivery in an ever-evolving technological environment. Welcome to a new era of programming and security—welcome to Groovy.

# Chapter 1: Introduction to Groovy and DevSecOps

In a time characterized by rapid software development and deployment, the need for agile methodologies has significantly increased. As organizations adopt DevOps practices, the integration of security measures throughout the software development lifecycle has become essential. This integration has led to the emergence of a new framework known as DevSecOps. Concurrently, the programming language Groovy has gained considerable popularity among developers due to its flexibility and effectiveness. This chapter delves into the fundamentals of Groovy and the core principles of DevSecOps, laying the groundwork for a comprehensive understanding of their convergence and practical uses.

### 1.1 Understanding Groovy

Groovy is an object-oriented programming language tailored for the Java platform, aimed at boosting developer efficiency. It seeks to offer a more expressive and dynamic coding experience while maintaining compatibility with existing Java libraries and frameworks. The syntax of Groovy is both concise and familiar to those with Java experience, making it an appealing option for developers aiming to optimize their coding workflow.**1.1.1 Key Features of Groovy:**

**Dynamic Typing:** Unlike Java, which enforces strict type checking, Groovy is dynamically typed. This feature allows developers to write code more quickly and flexibly, reducing boilerplate code and enhancing readability.

**Closures:** Groovy supports closures, which enable

developers to define blocks of code that can be executed at a later time. This feature empowers functional programming paradigms and allows for more elegant code patterns.

**GDK (Groovy Development Kit):** The GDK extends the Java SDK with additional methods and capabilities, empowering developers with a rich set of tools that simplify everyday coding tasks.

**Integration with Java:** Groovy's seamless interoperability with Java means that developers can leverage existing Java codebases while enjoying Groovy's innovative features. This capability makes Groovy ideal for projects that require rapid development without the need for a full rewrite.

Given these attributes, Groovy has become a popular choice for scripting, testing, and building applications, particularly within the realm of continuous integration and deployment.

### 1.2 The Rise of DevOps

DevOps is a cultural and technical movement that emphasizes collaboration between development and operations teams to enhance the deployment process. By breaking down silos and fostering a culture of shared responsibility, organizations can accelerate the delivery of software while maintaining high-quality standards. The core principles of DevOps include:

**Collaboration:** Encouraging teams to work together throughout the development cycle, from planning and development to deployment and monitoring.

**Automation:** Leveraging tools and scripts to reduce

manual intervention, streamline processes, and minimize the potential for human error.

**Continuous Feedback:** Implementing feedback loops that provide insights into performance, errors, and user experiences, allowing teams to iterate rapidly.

As companies embraced DevOps practices, the need for integrating security into the process became glaringly apparent. Traditional approaches often relegated security to the final stages of development, leading to vulnerabilities that could compromise systems after deployment. This realization paved the way for the emergence of DevSecOps.

### 1.3 The DevSecOps Evolution

DevSecOps is the practice of integrating security principles within the DevOps framework, ensuring that security is considered from the outset rather than as an afterthought. The goal of DevSecOps is to create a culture where everyone involved in the software development lifecycle is responsible for security, enhancing the overall security posture of the organization.

**1.3.1 Fundamental Principles of DevSecOps:**

**Shift Left:** This principle advocates for addressing security at the earliest stages of development. By implementing security practices during design and development, organizations can identify and remediate vulnerabilities before they become costly issues in production.

**Automation of Security Processes:** Just as DevOps teams automate deployment processes, DevSecOps encourages the automation of security checks, such as static code analysis, vulnerability scanning, and compliance audits. Tools like Jenkins, CircleCI, or GitLab CI can integrate security tests into the continuous integration pipeline seamlessly.

**Continuous Monitoring:** Once an application is deployed, continuous monitoring and assessment are crucial. This includes tracking security flaws, incidents, and compliance issues in real-time to ensure urgent threats are addressed promptly.

### 1.4 The Synergy Between Groovy and DevSecOps

The integration of Groovy within DevSecOps practices can enhance developers' ability to automate security processes and create scripts that guard against vulnerabilities swiftly. Groovy's concise syntax and expansive library support allow teams to build custom security tools and automate tests efficiently, thus contributing to the overall goals of DevSecOps.

As organizations increasingly adopt microservices architectures and containerization, Groovy's compatibility with popular frameworks like Spring Boot and its ability to write Jenkins pipelines further solidifies its role in the DevSecOps landscape.

Groovy's expressive syntax and dynamic features position it as an effective language for enhancing development processes, while the principles of DevSecOps call for a collaborative approach to security.

# Groovy Programming and DevSecOps Fundamentals

This chapter delves into the foundational aspects of Groovy programming, an agile and dynamic scripting language for the Java platform, and explores how it integrates with the DevSecOps philosophy. By understanding Groovy and DevSecOps fundamentals, developers can enhance their coding practices and ensure that security is embedded throughout the software development lifecycle (SDLC).

## Section 1: Groovy Programming Fundamentals ### 1.1 What is Groovy?

Groovy is an object-oriented programming language that runs on the Java Virtual Machine (JVM). It is designed to be a companion to Java, providing additional features that make it more concise and expressive while being fully interoperable with Java code. Groovy's syntax is similar to Java, which helps Java developers quickly adopt it.

### 1.2 Key Features of Groovy

**Dynamic Typing**: Unlike Java, Groovy allows for dynamic type checking, which can lead to shorter and more readable code.

**Closures**: Groovy supports closures, enabling developers to create blocks of code that can be executed later, enhancing functional programming capabilities.

**Native Collections**: Groovy provides powerful collection manipulation capabilities that simplify working with data structures.

**Metaprogramming**: The language's

metaprogramming features allow manipulation of classes and methods at runtime, enabling developers to build flexible and reusable code.

### 1.3 Setting Up a Groovy Development Environment

To get started with Groovy, developers can set up their environment easily:

**Install Java Development Kit (JDK)**: Ensure that JDK 8 or higher is installed.

**Install Groovy**: Download the Groovy binaries from the official website and set up environment variables accordingly.

**IDE Support**: Use an Integrated Development Environment (IDE) such as IntelliJ IDEA or Eclipse with the Groovy plugin for enhanced development features.

### 1.4 Basic Syntax and Examples

```groovy
// A simple Groovy script def greet(name) {
return "Hello, ${name}!"
}
println(greet("World")) // Output: Hello, World!
```

In this example, Groovy's ability to interpolate variables in strings showcases its syntactic simplicity and readability.

## Section 2: Introduction to DevSecOps ### 2.1 What is DevSecOps?

DevSecOps is a philosophy aimed at integrating security practices within the DevOps process. It transforms the traditional point-in-time security check into a continuous, integrated part of the development workflow. The goal is to foster a culture of security awareness and responsibility at every stage of the SDLC.

### 2.2 The Importance of DevSecOps

**Shift-left Security**: Engaging security earlier in the development process helps identify and mitigate vulnerabilities before they reach production.

**Collaboration**: DevSecOps requires collaboration between development, operations, and security teams, breaking down silos and encouraging shared responsibility.

**Automation**: Automating security testing and compliance checks is essential to delivering secure applications at speed without sacrificing quality.

### 2.3 Key Principles of DevSecOps

**Automation of Security**: Integrate automated security tools into CI/CD pipelines for real-time feedback on security postures.

**Continuous Monitoring**: Implement monitoring solutions that provide continuous insight into application behavior and potential exploits.

**Security as Code**: Treat security policies and

15

configurations as code, making them version-controlled, reviewable, and repeatable.

## Section 3: Integrating Groovy with DevSecOps ### 3.1 Using Groovy in CI/CD Pipelines

Groovy plays a pivotal role in automating DevSecOps processes, especially within CI/CD pipelines utilizing Jenkins, one of the most popular orchestration tools.

#### Example: Jenkins Pipeline Script in Groovy

```groovy
```groovy pipeline {
agent any stages {
stage('Build') { steps {
script {
// Build commands here
}
}
}
stage('Test') { steps {
script {
sh 'run_unit_tests.sh'
// Include security scanning commands here
```
```

```
}
}
}
stage('Deploy') { steps {
script {
// Deployment commands here
}
}
}
}
post {
failure {
// Security alert notifications
}
}
}
```
```

In this example, Groovy is used to define the stages of a Jenkins pipeline, incorporating security testing alongside other key processes.

### 3.2 Integrating Security Tools

Groovy can also facilitate the integration of security tools by providing scripts to automate static analysis, dependency scanning, and vulnerability detection within the CI/CD pipeline.
```

**Static Application Security Testing (SAST)**: Utilizing static analysis tools can identify vulnerabilities in code before deployment.

**Dynamic Application Security Testing (DAST)**: Performing dynamic tests against running applications to uncover runtime issues.

### 3.3 Creating a Secure Development Culture

Implementing DevSecOps with Groovy extends beyond technical practices. It requires:

**Training**: Educate teams on secure coding practices and Groovy capabilities.

**Culture**: Foster an environment where security is everyone's responsibility.

**Tools**: Leverage Groovy's flexibility to create custom security checks that align with specific project needs.

Groovy simplifies coding and enhances productivity while seamlessly integrating with various DevSecOps practices to ensure security is a fundamental component of the development workflow. By adopting Groovy in your development processes and embracing the principles of DevSecOps, you can build robust, secure applications that meet the demands of modern software delivery. As we continue to advance in these fields, embracing the synergy between development, security, and operations will remain crucial for success.

## Understanding DevSecOps Principles

This chapter delves into the principles of DevSecOps, a paradigm that combines development, security, and operations to deliver software faster while ensuring security is embedded throughout the lifecycle.

## 1. The Need for DevSecOps

Historically, development and security were often siloed, leading to long delays in the software delivery process and an increase in vulnerabilities. Development teams focused on speed and functionality, while security teams primarily concerned themselves with risk management and compliance. This dichotomy resulted in security being an afterthought—a reactive measure rather than a proactive strategy. As cyber threats have become more sophisticated, this traditional approach has proven insufficient.

DevSecOps emerges as a response to these challenges, promoting a culture of collaboration among development, operations, and security teams. By incorporating security practices early in the development process, organizations can build resilient software that not only meets functional requirements but also addresses security concerns from the outset.

## 2. Key Principles of DevSecOps

### 2.1 Continuous Integration and Continuous Deployment (CI/CD)

At the heart of DevSecOps is the CI/CD pipeline, where code changes are automatically tested and deployed to production. Integrating security checks at every stage of this pipeline ensures vulnerabilities are identified and addressed promptly. Automated testing tools can assess code for security flaws, enabling teams to remediate issues before they reach production.

### 2.2 Shift Left Strategy

The "shift left" approach emphasizes moving security practices to the earliest stages of the software development lifecycle. Instead of waiting until the end of the development process to conduct security testing, DevSecOps promotes the idea of addressing security from day one. This proactive strategy minimizes risks and reduces the costs associated with fixing vulnerabilities later in the lifecycle.

### 2.3 Collaboration and Communication

Effective collaboration among development, security, and operations teams is crucial for the success of DevSecOps. Open lines of communication foster shared understanding and collective ownership of security responsibilities. Regular meetings, joint training sessions, and shared tools can cultivate a culture where security is everyone's responsibility, preventing the "us versus them" mentality that can hinder progress.

### 2.4 Automation

Automation plays a vital role in DevSecOps, as it allows teams to integrate security testing into their existing workflows without disrupting productivity. By automating security tasks—such as code scanning, compliance checks, and vulnerability assessments—organizations can achieve greater efficiency and consistency. Automated responses to security incidents also allow teams to address threats in real time, significantly reducing the potential impact.

### 2.5 Continuous Monitoring and Feedback

Implementing DevSecOps is not a one-time effort; it requires ongoing monitoring and iteration. Continuous monitoring of applications in production enables organizations to detect and respond to security threats promptly. Feedback loops facilitate learning and improvement, encouraging teams to refine their processes and tools to enhance security over time.

## 3. Cultural Shifts

Embracing DevSecOps often necessitates a cultural transformation within organizations. Changing attitudes towards security, encouraging experimentation, and fostering a blame-free environment are paramount.

When teams view mistakes as opportunities for growth rather than failures, they are more likely to take ownership of security practices and innovate in their approaches.

This cultural shift must be supported by leadership that prioritizes security and allocates resources to training and tooling. By championing DevSecOps principles from the top down, organizations can create a robust framework that integrates security into every facet of their operations.

## 4. Challenges and Solutions

While implementing DevSecOps offers numerous benefits, organizations may face challenges, including resistance to change, skill gaps, and tool integration issues. Addressing these challenges requires a strategic approach:

**Managing Resistance to Change**: Engage stakeholders early in the process, communicate the benefits of DevSecOps, and involve them in decision-making to cultivate buy-in.


**Bridging Skill Gaps**: Invest in training programs and

workshops to enhance the skills of development, operations, and security teams. A focus on cross-functional training can also foster collaboration and understanding across disciplines.


**Choosing the Right Tools**: Select tools that integrate well with existing workflows. Prioritize solutions that support automation and provide comprehensive visibility across the development lifecycle.

DevSecOps principles guide organizations in transforming their approach to software development, creating a proactive security posture that enhances resilience. By adopting these principles, organizations not only protect their assets but also foster innovation and agility in delivering high-quality software. As we progress in our journey, the integration of development, security, and operations will be pivotal in navigating the complexities of the digital landscape and ensuring a secure future for all.

# Chapter 2: Setting Up Your Environment

DevSecOps emphasizes a culture of shared responsibility, enabling security practices to be seamlessly integrated into the DevOps pipeline. In this chapter, we'll explore how to set up your development environment in Groovy, one of the popular programming languages used for scripting and automation, to support these DevSecOps practices.

## 1. Understanding Groovy and Its Role

Groovy is a powerful, agile, and dynamic language that is built on the Java platform. Its syntax is similar to Java, making it more accessible for Java developers while providing additional features that enhance productivity. With its capabilities for scripting, domain-specific languages, and seamless integration with various Java libraries, Groovy is an ideal choice for automating DevSecOps tasks.

### 1.1 Benefits of Using Groovy in DevSecOps

**Simplicity**: Groovy's syntax is concise and expressive, allowing for quicker code writing and easier maintenance.

**Integration**: Groovy seamlessly integrates with existing Java libraries, REST APIs, and other tools within your development environment.

**Support for Domain-Specific Languages (DSLs)**: Groovy's flexibility allows teams to create DSLs tailored to specific security tasks, making automation more intuitive.

## 2. Setting Up Your Environment

Setting up your environment is the first step toward leveraging Groovy for DevSecOps practices. Below, we'll walk through the key components to ensure a fully functioning Groovy environment.

### 2.1 Installing Groovy

To start using Groovy, you first need to install it on your machine. Follow these steps:

**Download Groovy**: Visit the [Apache Groovy website](https://groovy.apache.org/download.html) and choose the latest distribution package.

**Install Groovy**:

For **Windows**: Extract the downloaded ZIP file and add the `bin` directory to your system's PATH environment variable.

For **Mac** or **Linux**: You can leverage SDKMAN! for easier installation. If SDKMAN! is not installed, follow the [installation guide](https://sdkman.io/install), then run:

```bash
sdk install groovy
```

**Verify Installation**: Open your terminal or command prompt and type:

```bash
groovy -version
```

If installed correctly, you'll see the Groovy version displayed. ### 2.2 Setting Up an Integrated Development

24

Environment (IDE)

While Groovy can be coded in any text editor, using a dedicated IDE can greatly enhance your development experience. Popular IDEs for Groovy include IntelliJ IDEA and Eclipse with the Groovy plugin.

**IntelliJ IDEA**:

Download the Community or Ultimate edition from the [JetBrains website](https://www.jetbrains.com/idea/download/).

During installation, ensure you include the Groovy plugin.

**Eclipse**:

Download Eclipse from the [Eclipse website](https://www.eclipse.org/downloads/).

Install the Groovy plugin via the Eclipse Marketplace. ### 2.3 Configuring Build Tools

In a DevSecOps environment, automation of builds, tests, and deployments is crucial. Most commonly, Gradle or Maven are used as build tools which naturally support Groovy.

#### Setting Up Gradle

**Install Gradle**: You can download and install Gradle from the [Gradle website](https://gradle.org/install/). Alternatively, you can use SDKMAN!:

```bash
sdk install gradle
```

**Create a Gradle Project**:

Navigate to your desired project location in the terminal and run:

```bash
gradle init --type groovy-application
```

This command sets up a basic Groovy application structure, complete with a build.gradle file. #### Setting Up Maven

**Install Maven**: Download Maven from the [Maven website](https://maven.apache.org/download.cgi) and set up your environment similar to Gradle.

**Create a Maven Project**:

Run the following Maven command to create a new project:

```bash
mvn                archetype:generate          -
DgroupId=com.yourcompany.devsecops           -
DartifactId=devsecops-groovy                 -
DarchetypeArtifactId=maven-archetype-quickstart   -
DinteractiveMode=false
```

### 2.4 Incorporating Security Tools

A key part of implementing DevSecOps is incorporating security tools into your workflow. The following are popular tools that can be integrated into your Groovy environment:

26

**OWASP Dependency-Check**: A tool to identify project dependencies and check for known vulnerabilities. Integrate it with Gradle or Maven to automate security checks.

**SonarQube**: A continuous inspection tool that tracks code quality and security vulnerabilities. You can set it up to analyze your Groovy code.

**Snyk**: An additional security scanner that specializes in identifying vulnerabilities within open-source libraries.

## 3. Writing Your First Groovy Script

Having set up the environment, let's write a simple Groovy script to demonstrate automation in a security context. Below is an example of a script that scans for vulnerable dependencies using OWASP Dependency-Check.

```groovy
// dependency-check.groovy def scan() {

def command = "dependency-check.sh --project 'DevSecOpsDemo' --scan ./path/to/your/project" def process = command.execute()

process.waitForProcessOutput(System.out, System.err) if(process.exitValue() == 0) {

println "Dependency scan completed successfully."

} else {

println "Dependency scan failed."

}

}
```

```
scan()
```
```
` ` `
```

In this chapter, you learned how to set up a Groovy environment tailored for DevSecOps practices. By installing Groovy, configuring your IDE, incorporating essential build tools, and integrating security tools into your workflow, you are well on your way to developing secure applications from the start. The next chapter will delve deeper into creating automated security tests with Groovy, further solidifying your DevSecOps foundation.

# Essential Tools and Plugins for Groovy Scripting

In this chapter, we will explore essential tools and plugins that can elevate your Groovy scripting experience, making it more efficient and enjoyable.

## 1. Integrated Development Environments (IDEs) ### 1.1 IntelliJ IDEA

IntelliJ IDEA is a favored IDE among Groovy developers, offering comprehensive support for Groovy language features. Its smart code completion, powerful refactoring tools, and built-in Groovy console make it a go-to tool for scripting. The integration with Gradle, along with advanced debugging features, allows developers to manage dependencies and troubleshoot scripts easily.

#### Key Features:

Built-in Groovy support and syntax highlighting.

Integrated unit testing tools (Spock, JUnit).

Version control system integrations (Git, SVN).

Plugins for enhanced framework support (Grails, Micronaut). ### 1.2 Eclipse with Groovy Eclipse Plugin

Eclipse is another popular choice among developers. The Groovy-Eclipse Plugin enhances the standard Eclipse environment, adding Groovy capabilities. This plugin provides effective syntax highlighting, compilation, and debugging features, making it easier to work with Groovy scripts.

#### Key Features:

Full support for Groovy syntax and features.

Project management capabilities and builder integration.

Support for Maven and Gradle build systems.

Debugging tools that cater to Groovy scripts. ### 1.3 Visual Studio Code

Visual Studio Code (VS Code) has established itself as a lightweight but powerful code editor. The Groovy extension for VS Code makes it a viable option for Groovy scripting. With features such as IntelliSense, snippets, and debugging capabilities, it can be a great environment for scripting in Groovy.

#### Key Features:

Syntax highlighting and code completion.

Integrated terminal for script execution.

Version control and collaborative features via extensions.

Customizable user interface and extension marketplace. ## 2. Build Tools

### 2.1 Gradle

As a popular build automation tool, Gradle supports Groovy natively, making it an essential part of the Groovy ecosystem. Gradle allows developers to define and manage project structures, dependencies, and build processes using Groovy-based build scripts.

#### Key Features:

Dependency management with an intuitive DSL.

Multi-project build capabilities.

Customizable build workflows and tasks using Groovy.

Integration with popular IDEs for seamless development.
### 2.2 Apache Maven

Maven is another build automation tool that is widely used in the Java ecosystem. With the Groovy-Eclipse Plugin, you can effectively utilize Groovy scripts in a Maven-managed project, benefiting from dependency management and build lifecycle automation.

#### Key Features:

Dependency management through a centralized POM file.

Easy integration of Groovy scripts as Maven goals.

Plugins to run Groovy scripts as part of the build process.
## 3. Testing Frameworks

### 3.1 Spock Framework

Spock is a Groovy-based testing and specification framework that is highly regarded for its expressive syntax and powerful features. It allows developers to write clear and concise tests, making it an essential tool for unit testing Groovy scripts.

#### Key Features:

DSL for writing tests and specifications.

Built-in support for mocking and spying.

Integration with popular continuous integration (CI) systems.

Compatibility with JUnit for older Java projects. ### 3.2 Geb

Geb is a powerful browser automation and testing tool built on top of Groovy. It's especially useful for testing web applications and supports various web automation frameworks. Geb's fluent API and easy integration with Spock make it a valuable asset for front-end testing.

#### Key Features:

Simplified browser automation with Groovy DSL.

Support for multiple browsers (Chrome, Firefox, etc.).

Easy integration with Spock for behavior-driven development. ## 4. Plugins and Libraries

### 4.1 Groovy-JSON

This built-in library simplifies working with JSON data in Groovy, enabling easy parsing and generation of JSON objects. It eliminates the need for external libraries, making data exchange with web services straightforward.

### 4.2 Apache Commons

The Apache Commons library suite provides reusable Java components and includes modules that can enhance Groovy scripts, such as `Commons Lang`, `Commons

IO`, and `Commons Collections`. Leveraging these libraries can save time and reduce boilerplate code. ### 4.3 Gradle Plugins

Many community-maintained Gradle plugins offer added functionality for Groovy projects. Examples include plugins for code quality checks, static analysis tools, and more, which help in maintaining a healthy codebase.

Whether you choose a robust IDE, a powerful build tool, or a specialized testing framework, each tool brings something unique to your development environment. As you become more familiar with these tools, your ability to write clean, effective scripts will enhance, allowing you to focus on what truly matters: creating solutions that work. In the following chapters, we will delve deeper into practical applications of Groovy scripting, providing you with hands-on examples to solidify your learning.

# Chapter 3: Groovy Fundamentals for Security Automation

As an agile language that runs on the JVM (Java Virtual Machine), Groovy not only leverages existing Java libraries but also introduces a concise syntax that minimizes boilerplate code. This chapter will delve into the fundamentals of Groovy, laying the groundwork necessary for automating security tasks effectively.

## 3.1 Why Groovy for Security Automation?

Groovy's unique characteristics make it an ideal choice for security automation:

**Interoperability with Java**: Groovy seamlessly integrates with Java, enabling security teams to utilize existing Java libraries and leverage a vast ecosystem of tools.

**Dynamic Typing**: This feature allows developers to write code more quickly without the need for extensive type definitions, making prototyping exceptionally fast.

**Simplified Syntax**: Groovy reduces boilerplate code, resulting in more readable and maintainable scripts. This is crucial for security automation, where clarity is essential for identifying vulnerabilities or performing audits.

**Built-in Support for Domain-Specific Languages (DSLs)**: Groovy facilitates the creation of DSLs, allowing teams to express complex security policies and processes in a syntax that is intuitive for non- developers.

## 3.2 Setting Up the Environment

Before diving into Groovy scripting, it is vital to set up the environment. Here are the steps to get started:

**Install Java**: Ensure that you have Java Development Kit (JDK) installed. You can download it from the [Oracle website](https://www.oracle.com/java/technologies/javase-jdk11-downloads.html) or use OpenJDK.

**Install Groovy**: Download and install Groovy from the [Groovy website](https://groovy-lang.org/download.html). Ensure that the Groovy executable is included in your system's PATH.

**Verify the Installation**: Open your terminal or command prompt and run the following commands:

```bash
groovy -version
```

You should see the installed version of Groovy confirming a successful setup.

**Choosing an IDE**: While you can write Groovy scripts in a basic text editor, using an IDE like IntelliJ IDEA or Eclipse can enhance productivity with features like syntax highlighting, code completion, and built- in debugging tools.

## 3.3 Basic Groovy Syntax

Understanding the fundamental syntax of Groovy is essential for effective scripting. Below are some basic constructs:

### 3.3.1 Variables and Data Types

Groovy is dynamically typed, allowing for flexible variable declarations. For example:

```groovy
def name = "SecurityAutomation" def age = 5
def isActive = true
```

### 3.3.2 Control Structures

Groovy supports control structures similar to Java, such as `if`, `else`, `for`, and `while`. Here's how to use an `if` statement:

```groovy
if (isActive) {
println "Automation is active."
} else {
println "Automation is not active."
}
```

### 3.3.3 Collections

Groovy offers powerful collection capabilities with lists, maps, and sets. Here's how to work with a list:

```groovy
def users = ["Alice", "Bob", "Charlie"] users.each { user ->
println user
}
```

### 3.3.4 Closures

Closures in Groovy are blocks of code that can be assigned to variables and executed later. They are particularly useful for callbacks and iterating over collections:

```groovy
def greet = { name -> println "Hello, ${name}!"
}

greet("Alice") // Output: Hello, Alice!
```

## 3.4 Groovy for Security Automation

With the fundamentals covered, let's look at how to apply Groovy skills in the context of security automation tasks.

### 3.4.1 Automation Scripts

Security teams can write automation scripts for tasks such as log parsing, vulnerability scanning, and incident response. Here's an example of a simple script to scan for specific keywords in log files:

```groovy
def logFile = new File('/var/log/security.log') def keywords = ['ERROR', 'CRITICAL', 'FAIL']


logFile.eachLine { line ->

if (keywords.any { line.contains(it) }) { println "Alert: ${line}"
}
}
```

### 3.4.2 Integrating with Security Tools

Groovy can be used to interact with various security tools via their APIs. Here's an example of how to use Groovy to send an alert to a security monitoring service:

```groovy
def sendAlert(message) {

def url = "https://monitoring-service.com/api/alerts" def json = new groovy.json.JsonBuilder()

json {

alert message

}

def connection = url.toURL().openConnection() connection.setRequestMethod("POST") connection.setDoOutput(true)

connection.getOutputStream().write(json.toString().getBytes("UTF-8")) def response = connection.content.text

println "Response: ${response}"

}

sendAlert("Suspicious activity detected!")
```

### 3.4.3 Creating DSLs for Security Policies

One of Groovy's powerful features is the ability to create DSLs. A security team could define a language for specifying firewall rules or compliance checks, making policy writing more accessible.

```groovy
firewall {
```

```
allow '192.168.1.1'
deny '192.168.1.100'
log 'ALL'
}
```
```

## 3.5 Best Practices for Groovy Security Automation

As you embark on using Groovy for security automation, consider these best practices:

**Maintain Code Clarity**: Use meaningful variable and method names to ensure that scripts are easy to understand and maintain.

**Use Version Control**: Even for small scripts, use a version control system like Git to track changes and collaborate with team members.

**Implement Error Handling**: Proper error handling can mitigate risks associated with unscripted failures. Use `try-catch` blocks where necessary.

**Test Regularly**: Regularly test your automation scripts in a controlled environment to ensure they perform as intended and do not introduce vulnerabilities.

**Leverage Community Resources**: Utilize Groovy communities and forums for resources, examples, and support as they can be invaluable in debugging and improving your scripts.

From setting up the environment to writing basic scripts, we uncovered how Groovy can streamline security tasks,
```

enabling teams to respond to threats swiftly and efficiently. In the next chapter, we will dive deeper into specific security automation scenarios, showcasing how Groovy can be used to solve real-world challenges.

# Key Groovy Features for DevSecOps Use Cases

DevSecOps merges development, security, and operations, ensuring that security is embedded from the outset. Groovy, a powerful, agile, and dynamic language for the Java Virtual Machine (JVM), presents several features that facilitate the implementation of DevSecOps practices. This chapter delves into the key Groovy features that make it an ideal choice for enhancing security in DevSecOps use cases.

## 1. Seamless Integration with Java Ecosystem

Groovy maintains full compatibility with Java, allowing practitioners to leverage existing Java libraries and tooling. This interoperability is crucial for DevSecOps, as it means teams can utilize mature security libraries such as Apache Shiro for authentication or OWASP ESAPI for security controls without rewriting existing modules. This capability enables quick integration of security measures into existing applications, promoting a secure coding environment.

### Use Case Example

A development team looking to incorporate security features can easily import and use Java-based security libraries within their Groovy scripts, avoiding the overhead of language incompatibility while maximizing functionality.

## 2. Domain-Specific Language (DSL) Capabilities

One of Groovy's standout features is its ability to create Domain-Specific Languages (DSLs). These DSLs enable teams to define security policies, configuration management, and deployment processes in a clear, expressive manner. By using DSLs, security teams can outline their requirements succinctly, making it easier for developers to implement necessary controls without navigating complex security protocols.

### Use Case Example

A security team might define a DSL for vulnerability scanning, allowing developers to easily configure and invoke scans within CI/CD pipelines. The DSL could simplify defining scan parameters and integrating results into the deployment process, ensuring vulnerabilities are addressed before production releases.

## 3. Closures and First-Class Functions

Groovy's support for closures—blocks of code that can be assigned to variables and passed around as first- class citizens—enables concise and flexible coding patterns. In a DevSecOps context, these closures can encapsulate security checks or validation functions, fostering reusable and clean security practices.

### Use Case Example

By using closures, a team could create reusable security validation functions to verify API inputs or configurations. These closures could be integrated into various parts of the application, ensuring consistent application of security across different modules without duplicating code.

## 4. Testing and Testing Frameworks

Groovy's integration with testing frameworks—most notably Spock—facilitates the writing of robust unit and integration tests. With the rise of automated testing as a component of DevSecOps, Groovy's syntax and concise test-writing capabilities allow teams to establish and enforce security policies in their testing

processes.

### Use Case Example

A development team could leverage Spock to write tests that specifically check for security vulnerabilities like SQL injection or XSS. By automating these tests within their CI/CD pipeline, they ensure that each code change adheres to security policies before being merged into production.

## 5. Dynamic Typing and MetaProgramming

Groovy's dynamic typing allows for rapid prototyping, facilitating quick iterations and changes. In the context of DevSecOps, this means teams can adjust security implementations and configurations quickly based on evolving threats without extensive refactoring.

MetaProgramming capabilities further enhance this flexibility, enabling developers to modify classes and methods at runtime to adapt security functionalities as needed. This can be useful in identifying and addressing security concerns without a full code deployment.

### Use Case Example

Security policies might change rapidly in response to emerging threats. Using Groovy's dynamic capabilities, a team can swiftly adjust security implementations, such as modifying authentication mechanisms or adjusting logging levels, ensuring a proactive security posture.

## 6. Built-in Support for Configuration Management

Groovy's ability to work seamlessly with configuration files and scripts makes it an outstanding choice for integrating security-related configurations. Frameworks such as Spring Boot benefit from Groovy's capabilities, allowing developers to manage application configurations dynamically and securely.

### Use Case Example

In a microservices architecture, configuration files can be managed with Groovy scripts that validate security settings, such as API keys and database credentials, at startup. This practice ensures that sensitive information is handled securely and consistently across services.

Groovy's features empower teams to implement security measures efficiently and effectively, promoting a culture that prioritizes secure coding practices. As organizations continue to pivot toward DevSecOps, the adoption of Groovy offers a strategic advantage, enabling rapid development cycles and enhanced security without compromising on quality or agility. By leveraging the discussed Groovy features, teams can navigate the complexities of modern software development while maintaining a robust security posture.

# Writing Your First Security Script in Groovy

With its concise syntax and powerful features, Groovy is particularly popular for writing scripts, building DSLs (domain-specific languages), and automating various tasks, including those related to security.

In this chapter, we'll walk through writing your first security script in Groovy. You'll learn about Groovy's syntax, familiarize yourself with some libraries relevant to security scripting, and implement a simple but effective security script that checks for potential security threats in your system.

## Setting Up Your Environment

Before diving into coding, it's essential to set up your Groovy development environment. You can run Groovy scripts using several methods, but for this chapter, we'll use two straightforward approaches:

**Install Groovy**: Download and install Groovy from the [official Groovy website](http://groovy-lang.org/download.html). Follow the installation instructions for your operating system.

**Using an IDE**: Although you can run Groovy scripts from the command line, using an IDE like IntelliJ IDEA or Eclipse can significantly enhance your development experience. Make sure to install the Groovy plugin for your IDE if needed.

Once Groovy is installed, you can verify it by typing `groovy -version` in your terminal or command prompt.

## Understanding the Basics of Groovy

Here's a quick overview of some Groovy basics that will be handy as we write our script:

**Syntax**: Groovy's syntax is quite close to Java but allows for more concise code without the need for boilerplate.

**Closures**: Groovy introduces closures, which are similar to lambda expressions in Java. They are blocks of code that can be assigned to variables or passed as parameters.

**Collections**: Groovy provides powerful support for Lists and Maps, making data management easier. ## Writing a Security Script

### Security Use Case: Log File Analyzer

In this section, we'll build a simple log file analyzer. This script will scan a log file for any occurrences of certain keywords that might indicate security threats, such as "ERROR," "FAILURE," or "EXCEPTION."

### Step 1: Setting Up the Script

Let's create a new Groovy script named `LogAnalyzer.groovy`. Open your favorite text editor or IDE and create the file.

### Step 2: Reading the Log File

Start by writing the code to read from a log file. We'll read the file line by line:

```groovy
// LogAnalyzer.groovy
```

```groovy
def logFile = new File('path/to/your/logfile.log') if
(!logFile.exists()) {

println "Log file does not exist." System.exit(1)

}

def threatKeywords = ["ERROR", "FAILURE",
"EXCEPTION"] def foundThreats = []

logFile.eachLine { line -> threatKeywords.each { keyword
->

if (line.contains(keyword)) { foundThreats << line

}

}

}
```
```

### Step 3: Displaying Results

Next, we'll display the lines that contain any of our threat
keywords:

```groovy
if (foundThreats.size() > 0) {

println "Potential security threats found:"
foundThreats.each { println it }

} else {

println "No threats found in the log file."

}
```

### Step 4: Putting It All Together

45
```

Your complete `LogAnalyzer.groovy` script looks like this:

```groovy
// LogAnalyzer.groovy

def logFile = new File('path/to/your/logfile.log') if (!logFile.exists()) {

println "Log file does not exist." System.exit(1)

}

def threatKeywords = ["ERROR", "FAILURE", "EXCEPTION"] def foundThreats = []

logFile.eachLine { line -> threatKeywords.each { keyword ->

if (line.contains(keyword)) { foundThreats << line

}

}

}


if (foundThreats.size() > 0) {

println "Potential security threats found:" foundThreats.each { println it }

} else {

println "No threats found in the log file."

}
```

### Step 5: Running Your Script

To run your script, navigate to the directory where your script resides, and execute the following command in your terminal:

```sh

groovy LogAnalyzer.groovy

```

Ensure your log file path is correct before running it. The script will output any lines from the log file that indicate potential security threats based on the specified keywords.

Congratulations! You've just written your first security script in Groovy. This simple log analyzer demonstrates how Groovy's concise syntax and powerful capabilities can help you automate security tasks effectively.

While this example focuses on log file analysis, Groovy can be used for much more complex security tasks, such as integrating with APIs, interacting with databases, and automating response actions.

# Chapter 4: Automating Security Audits with Groovy

In this chapter, we will delve into how Groovy, an agile and powerful programming language, can be utilized to automate security audits, streamline processes, and fortify defenses.

## 4.1 Introduction to Groovy

Groovy is an agile, dynamic language that runs on the Java platform. It seamlessly integrates with the Java environment and offers a concise syntax, making it an excellent choice for scripting and automation tasks. Its powerful features—such as closures, native syntax for lists and maps, and built-in support for regular expressions— allow developers to write expressive and efficient code. Furthermore, Groovy's interoperability with Java libraries and frameworks enables security professionals to leverage existing tools while implementing their automation scripts.

## 4.2 Understanding Security Audits

Before we explore how Groovy can automate security audits, it's important to understand the objectives of such audits. Security audits serve to evaluate the security policies, controls, and compliance of an organization's information systems. They help identify vulnerabilities, assess risks, and verify compliance with established regulations or standards. Common types of audits include:

**Internal Audits**: Conducted by internal teams to check adherence to policies.

**External Audits**: Performed by third parties for

independent assessments.

**Compliance Audits**: Ensure adherence to specific regulations like GDPR, HIPAA, or PCI-DSS.

By automating these audits, organizations can accelerate the process, reduce costs, and improve accuracy. ## 4.3 Key Benefits of Automating Security Audits with Groovy

### 4.3.1 Enhanced Efficiency

Automating tasks with Groovy allows security teams to focus on more strategic initiatives rather than manual, repetitive tasks. Scripts can run continuously, scanning systems and applications for vulnerabilities without requiring manual intervention.

### 4.3.2 Consistency and Accuracy

Human errors can lead to vulnerability overlooks. Automated scripts ensure that audits are performed in a consistent manner, reducing the risk of missing critical vulnerabilities and ensuring every test runs the same way each time.

### 4.3.3 Rapid Response

In the event of a detected vulnerability, automated systems can trigger alerts and even initiate remediation processes. This rapid response capability aids in minimizing the potential impact of security threats.

### 4.3.4 Improved Reporting

Groovy scripts can generate detailed reports dynamically, allowing security teams to quickly assess the status of their security posture. These reports can be customized to highlight specific compliance requirements or vulnerability trends.

## 4.4 Implementing Groovy Scripts for Security Audits
### 4.4.1 Setting Up the Environment

To get started with Groovy, ensure that you have the following tools installed:

**Java SDK**: Groovy runs on the Java Virtual Machine (JVM), so you need the Java Development Kit (JDK).

**Groovy**: Download and install Groovy from the official website.

**IDE**: While you can use any text editor, an Integrated Development Environment (IDE) like IntelliJ IDEA or Eclipse can enhance your coding experience with features like syntax highlighting and debugging tools.

### 4.4.2 Writing Basic Audit Scripts

To illustrate the power of Groovy in automating security audits, let's explore how to write a simple script that checks for open ports on a server.

```groovy
import java.net.*

def targetHost = "127.0.0.1" def ports = [22, 80, 443, 8080]

def checkPorts(host, ports) { ports.each { port ->

try {
```

```groovy
new Socket(host, port).close() println "Port ${port} is
open."
} catch (IOException e) {
println "Port ${port} is closed."
}
}
}
checkPorts(targetHost, ports)
```

This script attempts to connect to a series of ports on the
specified host and reports whether each port is open or
closed.

### 4.4.3 Scanning for Vulnerabilities

In a more advanced scenario, let's create a script that
integrates a vulnerability scanner API, fetching a report on
known vulnerabilities for specific applications.

```groovy
@Grab('org.codehaus.groovy.modules.http-builder:http-
builder:0.7.1') import groovyx.net.http.RESTClient

def client = new RESTClient('https://api.vulnerability-
scanner.com')

def response = client.get(path: '/scan', query: [target:
'example.com']) if (response.status == 200) {

def vulnerabilities = response.data.vulnerabilities if
(vulnerabilities) {

vulnerabilities.each { vulnerability ->
```

```
println  "Found  vulnerability:   ${vulnerability.title},
Severity: ${vulnerability.severity}"
}
} else {
println "No vulnerabilities found."
}
} else {
println "Error fetching vulnerabilities: ${response.status}"
}
```

This script uses an external API to check for vulnerabilities and can be easily customized to work with any vulnerability management tool that exposes an accessible API.

### 4.4.4 Scheduling Audits

For continuous security assessments, schedule your audit scripts to run at regular intervals using command- line jobs or task schedulers like `cron` in Unix-based systems. A simple cron job to run a Groovy script could look like this:

```bash
# Open crontab crontab -e
# Schedule script to run daily at midnight
0 0 * * * /path/to/groovy /path/to/securityAudit.groovy
```

## 4.5 Advanced Automation Techniques

While basic scripts are an excellent starting point, powerful automation often involves more complex workflows, such as integrating with configuration management tools (e.g., Ansible, Chef) or Continuous Integration/Continuous Deployment (CI/CD) pipelines.

### 4.5.1 Integrating with CI/CD Pipelines

Using Groovy in CI/CD tools, such as Jenkins, allows teams to incorporate security testing into the development pipeline:

```groovy
groovy pipeline {

agent any stages {

stage('Security Scan') { steps {

script {

sh 'groovy securityAudit.groovy'

}


}

}

}

}
```

This script triggers a security audit as part of the build process, ensuring that any vulnerabilities are detected prior to deployment.

### 4.5.2 Leveraging Groovy Libraries

Many Groovy libraries can assist in security audits.

Libraries like `OWASP ZAP` for web application security and `Apache Commons` for more functionality can be directly integrated into your scripts, further extending the capabilities of your audits.

In this chapter, we explored how Groovy can be a powerful ally in automating security audits, enhancing efficiency, consistency, and speed. By deploying Groovy scripts, organizations can not only reduce the manual effort involved in audits but also improve their security posture through proactive monitoring and rapid response.

# Building Scripts to Detect Vulnerabilities in Code

In the ever-evolving world of software development, securing applications from vulnerabilities has become an integral part of the development process. As languages like Java gain popularity, Groovy has emerged as a powerful, dynamic language that runs on the Java platform. Its concise syntax and seamless Java integration make it an attractive choice for developers. However, just like any other language, Groovy applications can also harbor vulnerabilities. In this chapter, we'll explore how to build scripts that automate the detection of vulnerabilities in code written in Groovy.

## Understanding Code Vulnerabilities

Before diving into the scripting process, it's crucial to understand what vulnerabilities are. In the context of programming, vulnerabilities refer to weaknesses in code that can be exploited by attackers to gain unauthorized access or cause harm. Common types of vulnerabilities include:

**Input Validation Flaws**: Failure to validate user inputs can lead to issues such as SQL Injection or Cross-Site Scripting (XSS).

**Insecure Deserialization**: Malicious data that is deserialized can lead to remote code execution.

**Sensitive Data Exposure**: Improper protection of sensitive information can lead to data breaches.

By detecting these vulnerabilities early in the development cycle, we can enhance the security posture of our applications.

## Setting Up Your Groovy Environment

To build effective scripts in Groovy, you need the following setup:

**Groovy Installation**: Ensure you have Groovy installed on your machine. You can download it from the [Groovy website](https://groovy-lang.org/download.html) and follow the installation instructions.


**IDE Support**: Use an IDE that supports Groovy, such as IntelliJ IDEA, Eclipse, or Visual Studio Code. They provide features such as syntax highlighting and error detection that can help in script development.

**Libraries for Vulnerability Detection**: Familiarize yourself with libraries that can assist in detecting vulnerabilities. Some popular ones include:

**OWASP Dependency-Check**: A tool for identifying project dependencies and checking them against a known database of vulnerabilities.

**FindBugs/SpotBugs**: A static analysis tool that can help identify potential vulnerabilities in Java and Groovy code.

## Writing Scripts to Detect Vulnerabilities

With your environment set up, it's time to write scripts. Let's go through some of the key vulnerability detection scripts, starting with detecting input validation flaws.

### Example 1: Detecting Input Validation Flaws

```groovy
import java.nio.file.*

import java.util.regex.*

def findInputValidationFailures(filePath) { def path = Paths.get(filePath)

def pattern = ~/.*request.*\['.*'\].*/ def lines = Files.readAllLines(path)

lines.eachWithIndex { line, index -> if (line =~ pattern) {

println "Potential input validation flaw at line ${index + 1}: ${line.trim()}"

}

}

}

findInputValidationFailures('src/main/groovy/MyApp.groovy')
```

This script scans a specified Groovy file for patterns that

indicate the use of unsanitized user input. It looks for lines where request parameters could potentially be directly used without validation, marking them for further review.

### Example 2: Detecting Sensitive Data Exposure

```groovy
def sensitivePatterns = [
~/.*password.*\s*:\s*.*?('.*?').*/,
~/.*secret.*\s*:\s*.*?('.*?').*/,
~/.*token.*\s*:\s*.*?('.*?').*/
]
def detectSensitiveData(filePath) { def path = Paths.get(filePath)
def lines = Files.readAllLines(path)
lines.eachWithIndex { line, index -> sensitivePatterns.each { pattern ->
if (line =~ pattern) {
println "[WARNING] Potential sensitive data exposure at line ${index + 1}: ${line.trim()}"
}
}
}
}
detectSensitiveData('src/main/groovy/MyApp.groovy')
```

This script checks for patterns in code that may reveal

sensitive information such as passwords or tokens. By identifying these instances, developers can take appropriate actions to secure sensitive data.

### Example 3: Integration with OWASP Dependency-Check

Integrating third-party tools enhances the power of your scripts. Here's a lightweight Groovy script to kick off an OWASP Dependency-Check scan:

```groovy
def executeDependencyCheck() {

def command = "dependency-check.sh --project MyApp --scan ./src --out ." def process = command.execute()

process.waitFor() println process.text

}

executeDependencyCheck()
```

This snippet executes an OWASP Dependency-Check scan and outputs vulnerabilities found in project dependencies that could be exploited.

## Testing and Refining Your Scripts

After developing your vulnerability detection scripts, it's essential to test and refine them. Consider the following best practices:

**Create a Test Suite**: Write test cases with known vulnerabilities to ensure your scripts can detect them reliably.

**Iterate Over Scripts**: Regularly update your detection logic based on new vulnerability findings and patterns.

**Feedback Loop**: Engage with developers to refine the criteria used in your scripts based on their feedback.

With the constant threat of cyber attacks, integrating security measures early in the development cycle is paramount. The scripts provided are foundational; they can be expanded with more complex logic and integrated into continuous integration pipelines to ensure ongoing security checks. As the landscape of vulnerabilities evolves, so too should our approaches to detecting and mitigating them, ensuring our Groovy applications remain robust and secure.

# Automating Dependency Scans and Reporting

With the rise of Groovy as a popular language for building applications, especially in environments like Jenkins and Gradle, automating dependency scans and reporting in Groovy has never been more important. This chapter will focus on how to set up automated dependency scans and generate insightful reports using Groovy.

## Understanding Dependency Management

Dependencies are external libraries or frameworks that your application relies on. Managing these dependencies accurately involves:

**Identifying** the libraries your application uses.

**Versioning** to ensure compatibility.

**Securing** to prevent vulnerabilities from outdated or malicious libraries.

**Documenting** to provide visibility into the software supply chain.

In a Groovy-based environment, tools like Gradle or Maven can be employed to manage these dependencies effectively. However, automating the processes of scanning these dependencies for issues and generating reports can save substantial time and effort, particularly in continuous integration/continuous deployment (CI/CD) pipelines.

## Tools for Dependency Scanning

Before diving into the automation part, it's important to understand some tools that can help in dependency scanning:

**OWASP Dependency-Check**: A tool that identifies project dependencies and checks if there are any known vulnerabilities.

**Gradle Dependency Audit Plugin**: A Gradle plugin that analyzes dependencies and produces a report.

**Custom Groovy Scripts**: For developers looking for specific customizations, Groovy scripts can be tailored to scan dependency files.

## Setting Up Dependency Scanning in Groovy

### Step 1: Incorporating Dependency Scanning Tools

To get started, you'll need to integrate a dependency

scanning tool into your Groovy project. For this example, we'll use OWASP Dependency-Check. You can include it in a Gradle build by adding the plugin:

```groovy
plugins {

id 'org.springframework.boot' version '2.5.4'

id 'io.spring.dependency-management' version '1.0.11.RELEASE' id 'org.owasp.dependencycheck' version '6.4.0'
}

repositories { mavenCentral()
}

dependencies {

implementation 'org.springframework.boot:spring-boot-starter'


// Other dependencies
}
```

### Step 2: Configuring the Plugin

Next, configure the OWASP Dependency-Check plugin by adding the following to your `build.gradle`:

```groovy
dependencyCheck {

failBuildOnCVSS = 5 // Fail the build on vulnerabilities with a CVSS score of 5 or higher reportFormat = 'ALL' // Generate multiple report formats (HTML, XML, etc.)
}
```

```
```

### Step 3: Running the Dependency Check

You can run Dependency-Check from the command line or your CI pipeline. Simply execute:

```
```

./gradlew dependencyCheckAggregate

```
```

This command will scan your project dependencies and generate an aggregated report, summarizing any vulnerabilities found.

## Automating Reporting with Groovy

Now that we have a dependency scan in place, the next step is to automate the reporting process. This could involve sending reports via email, generating dashboards, or logging the results into an external system.

### Step 1: Creating a Custom Reporting Script

Using Groovy, we can create a script that processes the generated report files. Below is a simple example to parse and print out the findings:

```groovy
def reportDir = new File('build/reports/dependency-check-report/') def reportFile = new File(reportDir, 'dependency-check-report.html')

if (reportFile.exists()) {

def reportContent = reportFile.text println "Dependency Scan Report:" println reportContent
```

```groovy
} else {

println "Report not found. Please ensure the scan was run."

}
```

### Step 2: Sending Reports via Email

To send the report via email, you can use Groovy's built-in `javax.mail` package. Below is an example method that sends the report via email:

```groovy
import javax.mail.*

import javax.mail.internet.*

void sendEmailReport(String recipient, String subject, String content) { Properties props = new Properties()

props.put("mail.smtp.host",          "smtp.example.com")
props.put("mail.smtp.port", "587")

Session session = Session.getInstance(props, null) try {

Message message = new MimeMessage(session)
message.setFrom(new InternetAddress("sender@example.com"))

message.setRecipients(Message.RecipientType.TO,
InternetAddress.parse(recipient,          false))
message.setSubject(subject)

message.setText(content)

Transport.send(message)
```

```
println "Report sent successfully to $recipient"
} catch (MessagingException e) { throw new
RuntimeException(e)
}
}
// Usage example
sendEmailReport("recipient@example.com",
"Dependency Scan Report", "Check the attached report for
details.")
```
```

## Integrating with CI/CD Pipelines

The setup described can be seamlessly integrated into
your CI/CD pipeline. You can use Jenkins, GitLab CI,
GitHub Actions, or any other tool of your choice:

**Trigger the scan** on each build or on a daily schedule.

**Generate reports** and send alerts for critical
vulnerabilities.

Use pipeline conditions to halt builds if critical
vulnerabilities are detected.

By leveraging existing tools and customizing them with
Groovy scripts, developers can ensure they remain one
step ahead of potential vulnerabilities and are well-
equipped to maintain the integrity of their software supply
chain. As development practices continue to evolve,
building automated systems will be key to ensuring robust
and secure applications.
```

# Chapter 5: Groovy in CI/CD Pipelines

This chapter explores the role of Groovy in CI/CD pipelines, discussing its syntax, benefits, and practical applications, while also providing examples to illustrate its power and flexibility.

## 5.1 Understanding CI/CD Pipelines

Before diving into Groovy, it's essential to understand the concepts of CI/CD. Continuous Integration involves integrating code changes into a shared repository several times a day, where automated tests are run to identify defects early. Continuous Delivery takes this a step further by ensuring that those code changes can be deployed to production at any time, using automated deployment push mechanisms.

CI/CD pipelines are essentially workflows that automate the software delivery process. These pipelines consist of various stages, including code compilation, testing, packaging, and deployment, which must be executed reliably and consistently.

## 5.2 The Role of Groovy in CI/CD

Groovy, an agile and dynamic language for the Java Virtual Machine (JVM), brings significant advantages to CI/CD processes:

**Declarative Syntax**: Groovy utilizes a concise and expressive syntax that allows developers to write less code while maintaining readability. This is particularly beneficial in CI/CD pipelines where clarity and brevity are crucial.

**Integration with Jenkins**: Jenkins, one of the most

popular CI/CD tools, leverages Groovy for its pipeline as code feature. Groovy scripts can directly control Jenkins jobs, enabling seamless integration and automation of the entire CI/CD workflow.

**Domain-Specific Language (DSL)**: Groovy allows developers to create DSLs, which can be tailor- made for specific needs within the pipeline, enhancing abstraction and modularity.

**Built-in Support for Java Libraries**: Since Groovy runs on the JVM, it can easily leverage Java libraries and frameworks, making it a powerful tool for developers already familiar with the Java ecosystem.

## 5.3 Setting Up a Groovy-Based Jenkins Pipeline

Let's explore how to create a simple Groovy-based Jenkins pipeline. The following example outlines a basic CI/CD pipeline for a Java application that includes stages for building, testing, and deploying.

### Step 1: Defining the Pipeline

Create a `Jenkinsfile` at the root of your project. This file will define the stages of your pipeline using Groovy DSL.

```groovy
pipeline {

agent any

stages {

stage('Build') { steps {

echo 'Building the application...'


sh './gradlew build' // Assuming a Gradle build system
```

```
        }
    }
    stage('Test') { steps {
    echo 'Running tests...' sh './gradlew test'
    }
    }
    stage('Deploy') { steps {
    echo 'Deploying to production...'
    sh 'ssh user@yourserver "cd /path/to/app && git pull &&
    ./deploy.sh"'
    }
    }
    }
}
```
```

### Step 2: Executing the Pipeline

With the `Jenkinsfile` in place, every time a change is pushed to the repository, Jenkins will automatically trigger the pipeline, executing each defined stage in sequence. If any stage fails, the pipeline will stop, and developers will be notified to investigate and rectify the issue.

## 5.4 Advanced Groovy Techniques in CI/CD

While basic pipelines are fantastic, Groovy offers numerous advanced features for optimizing and extending your CI/CD workflows.
```

### 5.4.1 Using Shared Libraries

In larger projects, you may want to share common scripts across multiple pipelines. Jenkins allows you to define Shared Libraries that encapsulate reusable code.

```groovy
@Library('my-shared-library') _
pipeline {
// use shared functions and classes
}
```

You can centralize helper functions, utility scripts, and configuration in a Git repository, promoting DRY (Don't Repeat Yourself) principles.

### 5.4.2 Dynamic Pipeline Generation

Groovy can also be used to generate pipeline stages dynamically based on certain conditions, configurations, or environment variables.

```groovy
def deployEnvironments = ['staging', 'production']

pipeline { agent any stages {
stage('Deploy to Environments') { steps {
deployEnvironments.each { env -> echo "Deploying to ${env}..."
// Deployment logic here
```

```
}
}
}
}
}
```
```

## 5.5 Debugging and Error Handling

Effective CI/CD pipelines require robust error handling and logging. Groovy provides several ways to implement error handling directly within your pipeline. Use try-catch blocks to gracefully handle failures and log messages to help with debugging.

```groovy
pipeline {

agent any stages {

stage('Build') { steps {

script {

try {

sh 'gradle build'

} catch (Exception e) {

echo "Build failed: ${e.message}" currentBuild.result = 'FAILURE'

}
}
}
}
```
```

```
}
}
```
\` \` \`

The integration of Groovy in CI/CD pipelines significantly enhances the development workflow, providing teams with the tools necessary to automate processes, increase collaboration, and maintain high code quality. By understanding and leveraging Groovy's features, developers can create powerful, maintainable, and scalable pipelines that adapt to changing business needs.

# Integrating Groovy Scripts into Jenkins Pipelines

This chapter will delve into the integration of Groovy scripts into Jenkins pipelines, focusing on how developers can leverage Groovy for improved control, flexibility, and functionality in their CI/CD workflows.

## Understanding Jenkins Pipelines

Jenkins uses a domain-specific language (DSL) based on Groovy to define pipelines, which are automated processes that arrange and sequence tasks and stages. A pipeline can be defined in two primary formats: Declarative and Scripted.

### Declarative Pipeline

A Declarative pipeline provides a more structured and simpler syntax, making it easier for users, especially those new to Jenkins or Groovy. The pipeline is defined using a series of blocks that represent different stages of the build.

```groovy
pipeline {
agent any stages {
stage('Build') { steps {
sh 'make'
}
}
stage('Test') { steps {
sh 'make test'
}
}
}
}
```

### Scripted Pipeline

On the other hand, a Scripted pipeline offers more flexibility and control but typically requires greater knowledge of Groovy syntax. This type of pipeline is built with various Groovy constructs, leading to more complex and dynamic integrations.

```groovy
node {
stage('Build') { sh 'make'
}
stage('Test') { sh 'make test'
}
```

```
}
```
```

## Why Use Groovy Scripts?

Integrating Groovy scripts into your Jenkins pipeline provides several advantages:

**Dynamic Behavior**: Groovy scripts can generate dynamic content, looping through environments, jobs, or parameters as necessary.

**Reusable Code**: Common operations can be encapsulated into Groovy functions, enabling code reuse within pipelines and across different jobs.

**Improved Readability**: Well-structured Groovy scripts can enhance the readability and maintainability of the Jenkins pipeline.

**Error Handling**: Groovy scripts can include robust error-handling capabilities to manage exceptions and failures elegantly.

**Access to Jenkins API**: Groovy enables direct access to the Jenkins API, allowing for sophisticated interactions with the Jenkins environment.

## Creating and Using Groovy Scripts in Jenkins ### Step 1: Writing a Groovy Script

Start by creating a Groovy script file (`myScript.groovy`). Below is a simple example that defines a function to greet a user based on a name parameter.

```groovy
```
```

```groovy
def greetUser(name) { return "Hello, ${name}!"
}
// Call the function
println greetUser('Jenkins User')
```

### Step 2: Integrating the Groovy Script into a Pipeline

You can utilize Groovy scripts in both Declarative and Scripted pipelines. Here's how you might invoke the script from a Declarative pipeline.

```groovy
pipeline {
agent any stages {
stage('Run Groovy Script') { steps {
script {
// Load and run the Groovy script def output = load 'myScript.groovy'
println output.greetUser('Jenkins User')
}
}
}
}
}
```

### Step 3: Using Shared Libraries

For larger projects, especially those with multiple Jenkins

jobs and pipelines, it's often beneficial to create a Shared Library. A Shared Library allows you to store your Groovy scripts in a centralized location within your version control system, making them accessible across different Jenkins projects.

#### Creating a Shared Library

**Structure Your Library**: Create a repository with the following structure:

```
(my-shared-library) vars

myScript.groovy
```

**Defining the Script in vars**: Within `myScript.groovy`, encapsulate the functionality needed across your Jenkins jobs.

```groovy
def call(String name) { return "Hello, ${name}!"

}
```

**Configuring Jenkins**: In Jenkins, go to Manage Jenkins > Configure System. Under the Global Pipeline Libraries section, add your Shared Library repository.

**Using the Shared Library in Your Pipeline**:

```groovy
@Library('my-shared-library') _

pipeline { agent any stages {
```

```
stage('Greet User') { steps {
script {
def greeting = myScript('Jenkins User') println greeting
}
}
}
}
}
```
```

## Best Practices for Using Groovy Scripts

**Keep It Simple**: Begin with straightforward scripts and gradually evolve complexity as needed.

**Log Messages**: Utilize Jenkins logging features to output important information, helping you debug issues quickly.

**Test Your Scripts**: Regularly test your Groovy scripts locally and within Jenkins to ensure they work as expected.

**Use Comments**: Adding comments can greatly enhance the clarity and maintainability of your scripts.

**Version Control**: Store your scripts in version control to facilitate collaboration and version management.

By leveraging Shared Libraries, you can maximize the efficiency of your development and deployment processes. As you continue to explore and utilize Groovy in Jenkins, you will find new ways to streamline automation and
```

improve collaboration within your teams.

# Automating Security Testing in CI/CD Workflows

This chapter will delve into how to automate security testing within CI/CD workflows using Groovy, a versatile scripting language that runs on the Java platform and is widely used in Jenkins pipelines.

## Understanding CI/CD and the Role of Security

CI/CD practices aim to shorten the development lifecycle while maintaining high software quality. Continuous Integration (CI) focuses on automatically testing and integrating code changes into a shared repository, while Continuous Deployment (CD) automates the release of those changes into production.

Security, often referred to as DevSecOps, plays a pivotal role in CI/CD by introducing security checks and balances at every stage of the software development lifecycle. By integrating automated security testing earlier in the process, teams can discover and remediate vulnerabilities before they reach production, reducing the risk of security breaches and other issues.

## Getting Started

### Tools for Security Testing

Before delving into Groovy scripting, it's essential to identify the security testing tools you want to integrate into your CI/CD pipeline. Common tools include:

**OWASP ZAP (Zed Attack Proxy)**: A popular open-source tool for finding vulnerabilities in web applications.

**SonarQube**: A tool that focuses on code quality and security vulnerabilities.

**Snyk**: A developer-friendly tool that scans for and fixes vulnerabilities in open source libraries.

**Checkmarx**: A static application security testing (SAST) solution.

Selecting the right tools will depend on your application architecture, the coding languages in use, and the specific security needs of your organization.

### Setting Up Jenkins

Jenkins, a widely-used open-source automation server, will be our platform for implementing CI/CD workflows. To proceed, ensure you have Jenkins installed and configured.

**Installation**: Follow the official Jenkins installation guide suitable for your operating system.

**Plugins**: Install necessary plugins such as the Groovy, Pipeline, and relevant security testing tools integrations.

## Implementing Security Testing with Groovy in Jenkins
### Creating a Jenkins Pipeline

Jenkins pipelines can be defined using a domain-specific language (DSL) based on Groovy. A typical pipeline consists of stages that represent different steps in the CI/CD process. Here's an example of a simple declarative pipeline that incorporates security testing:

```groovy
pipeline {
```

```
agent any
stages {
stage('Build') { steps {
// Build application
sh 'mvn clean package'
}
}

stage('Unit Tests') { steps {
// Execute unit tests sh 'mvn test'
}
}
stage('Security Testing') { steps {
script {
// Run OWASP ZAP security scanner
def zapResults = sh(script: 'zap-baseline.py -t
http://yourapp-url -r zap-report.html', returnStdout:
true)


echo "ZAP Results: ${zapResults}"
// Check for vulnerabilities in the report if
(zapResults.contains("Warning")) {
currentBuild.result = 'FAILURE'
```

```
                error("Security vulnerabilities found. Check the ZAP
report.")



}
}
}
}
stage('Deploy') { steps {
// Deploy application if no security issues sh
'deploy_script.sh'
}
}
}


post {
always {
// Archive the ZAP report for review archiveArtifacts
artifacts: 'zap-report.html'
}
}
}
```
```

### Explanation of the Pipeline
```

**Agent**: The pipeline runs on any available agent in the Jenkins environment.

**Stages**:

**Build**: Executes the build process using Maven.

**Unit Tests**: Runs unit tests to verify that the application behaves as expected.

**Security Testing**: This crucial stage employs OWASP ZAP by running a baseline scan against the application. If vulnerabilities are detected, the pipeline fails, and the build is marked as unsuccessful.

**Deploy**: This stage only executes if all previous stages are successful, ensuring that only secure code is deployed.

**Post Actions**: The pipeline archives the ZAP report, providing an artifact for further analysis by team members.

### Integrating Other Tools

The pipeline can be extended to include various security tools. For instance, incorporating SonarQube for static code analysis can happen in a new stage:

```groovy
stage('SonarQube Analysis') { steps {
script {
//          Run          SonarQube          analysis
withSonarQubeEnv('SonarQube_Server') {
sh 'mvn sonar:sonar'
}
```

```
        }
    }
}
```
` ` `

## Best Practices for Security Testing in CI/CD

**Shift Left**: Implement security testing as early as possible in the CI/CD pipeline.

**Automate**: Leverage automation to perform security scans with each code change.

**Prioritize Findings**: Not all vulnerabilities have the same level of risk. Use tools that enable you to prioritize vulnerabilities based on their severity.

**Educate the Teams**: Foster a security-oriented culture by educating developers and operational teams on secure coding practices.

**Monitor and Adapt**: Continuously monitor for new vulnerabilities and adapt your security testing approach accordingly.

Using Groovy in Jenkins pipelines streamlines the integration of security tools and creates a robust process for identifying vulnerabilities early in the development lifecycle. As organizations strive for faster releases and greater security assurance, leveraging Groovy for automation in CI/CD workflows will remain a cornerstone in the pursuit of secure software delivery.

# Chapter 6: Securing Infrastructure with Groovy

In this chapter, we will explore how Groovy, coupled with its powerful frameworks and libraries, can be utilized to effectively secure infrastructure. This will include techniques ranging from authentication and authorization to network security and data protection.

## Understanding the Basis of Infrastructure Security

Before diving into Groovy specifics, it is essential to understand the core principles of infrastructure security. The foundation rests on three fundamental pillars: Confidentiality, Integrity, and Availability (CIA). When applied properly, these principles can guide the implementation of a secure infrastructure.

**Confidentiality** ensures that sensitive information is accessed only by authorized individuals or systems.

**Integrity** maintains the accuracy and consistency of data, protecting it from unauthorized changes.

**Availability** guarantees that resources and data are accessible to authorized users when needed. ## Why Groovy for Security?

Groovy, as a dynamic language for the Java platform, provides various features that make it an attractive choice for implementing security measures. Its compatibility with Java libraries, concise syntax, and powerful scripting capabilities allow for rapid development and integration of security protocols without sacrificing performance.

### Key Security Features in Groovy

**Simplified Syntax and DSLs**: Groovy's syntax is more human-readable compared to Java, allowing developers to write complex security configurations more succinctly. Moreover, Groovy supports Domain Specific Languages (DSLs), which can be used to create custom security configurations that are both expressive and easy to manage.

**Integration with Spring Security**: The Spring ecosystem is widely adopted for building secure Java applications. Groovy seamlessly integrates with Spring, making it possible to leverage Spring Security's robust features, such as authentication, role-based access control, and secure session management with minimal boilerplate code.

**Scripting Flexibility**: Given Groovy's ability to execute scripts dynamically, it is ideal for implementing security automation tasks. For example, you can dynamically check user roles and permissions or trigger security events with just a few lines of code.

## Implementing Authentication and Authorization ### Setting Up Spring Security with Groovy

To illustrate how Groovy can be used to secure infrastructure, let's create a basic application that employs Spring Security for user authentication.

**Project Setup**: Start a new Groovy project using a build tool like Gradle or Maven. Ensure you include the necessary Spring Security dependencies.

```groovy dependencies {
implementation 'org.springframework.boot:spring-boot-starter-security'                    implementation 'org.springframework.boot:spring-boot-starter-web'
}
```

**Configuring Security**: Create a configuration class that extends `WebSecurityConfigurerAdapter` to manage security settings.

```groovy
import org.springframework.context.annotation.Configuration

import org.springframework.security.config.annotation.web.builders.HttpSecurity

import org.springframework.security.config.annotation.web.configuration.EnableWebSecurity

import org.springframework.security.config.annotation.web.configuration.WebSecurityConfigurerAdapter

@Configuration @EnableWebSecurity

class              SecurityConfig              extends WebSecurityConfigurerAdapter {

@Override

protected    void    configure(HttpSecurity    http)    {
http.authorizeRequests()
```

```
.antMatchers('/login').permitAll()
.anyRequest().authenticated()
.and()
.formLogin().loginPage('/login').permitAll()
.and()
.logout().permitAll()
    }
}
```
` ` `

In this configuration, we specify that all requests must be authenticated, except for the login page. ### User Authentication Logic

Next, you need to create a user detail service that loads user-specific data.

` ` `groovy

import org.springframework.security.core.userdetails.UserDetailsService

import org.springframework.security.core.userdetails.UsernameNotFoundException                import org.springframework.security.core.userdetails.UserDetails

import org.springframework.security.core.userdetails.User

class     CustomUserDetailsService     implements UserDetailsService { @Override

```groovy
UserDetails loadUserByUsername(String username) {
// Fetch the user from the database (mocked here) if
(username == "admin") {
return User.withUsername("admin")
.password("{noop}password")
.roles("ADMIN")
.build()
} else {
throw new UsernameNotFoundException("User not
found: " + username)
}
}
}
```

Here, we mock the user authentication process. In a real-world application, you would query a database or an external service.

## Securing Data with Encryption

Data protection is an integral part of securing infrastructure. Groovy can integrate with Java's extensive libraries for encryption and hashing. Here's how you can encrypt sensitive data before storing it in the database.

### Example of Using AES Encryption

```groovy
import javax.crypto.Cipher
```

```
import          javax.crypto.KeyGenerator          import
javax.crypto.SecretKey

import javax.crypto.spec.SecretKeySpec

class EncryptionUtil {

private static final String ALGORITHM = "AES"

SecretKey generateKey() {

KeyGenerator              keyGen              =
KeyGenerator.getInstance(ALGORITHM)
keyGen.init(128)

return keyGen.generateKey()

}

byte[] encrypt(String data, SecretKey key) {

Cipher   cipher   =   Cipher.getInstance(ALGORITHM)
cipher.init(Cipher.ENCRYPT_MODE, key)

return cipher.doFinal(data.getBytes())

}

String decrypt(byte[] encryptedData, SecretKey key) {
Cipher   cipher   =   Cipher.getInstance(ALGORITHM)
cipher.init(Cipher.DECRYPT_MODE, key)

return new String(cipher.doFinal(encryptedData))

}

}
```
```

In this example, we use AES (Advanced Encryption Standard) to encrypt and decrypt sensitive information, ensuring that only authorized parties can access it.
```

## Network Security Considerations

When securing infrastructure, it is also essential to consider network and application-layer protections. Groovy can be leveraged to configure secure communication protocols, such as HTTPS, and reinforce application firewalls and intrusion detection systems.

### Securing Communication with HTTPS

You should have a valid SSL/TLS certificate for your application server. In configurations, specify that HTTP requests should be redirected to HTTPS.

```groovy
import org.springframework.context.annotation.Configuration

import org.springframework.security.config.annotation.web.builders.HttpSecurity

import org.springframework.security.config.annotation.web.configuration.EnableWebSecurity

import org.springframework.security.config.annotation.web.configuration.WebSecurityConfigurerAdapter

@Configuration @EnableWebSecurity

class SecurityConfig extends WebSecurityConfigurerAdapter {

@Override

protected void configure(HttpSecurity http) {
http.requiresChannel()
```

```
.anyRequest().requiresSecure()

}

}
```
``` ` ` ```

In this configuration, we enforce that all requests must use secure channels.

Securing infrastructure is a multifaceted challenge that demands a comprehensive strategy. Groovy, empowered by its intuitive syntax and robust integration with security frameworks like Spring Security, offers an effective platform for implementing security best practices. Whether you are managing user authentication, protecting sensitive data, or securing network communication, Groovy's capabilities provide an efficient and flexible approach to infrastructure security.

## Writing Groovy Scripts for Cloud Security Audits

Organizations are increasingly relying on robust security audits to identify vulnerabilities and compliance gaps. Groovy, a powerful scripting language for the Java platform, has emerged as a valuable tool for automating cloud security audit processes. In this chapter, we will explore how to harness Groovy scripting to streamline and enhance cloud security audits, covering the fundamentals of Groovy, practical examples, and best practices for effective script development.

## 1. Understanding Groovy
```

Groovy is an agile and dynamic language that complements Java by providing a more concise and expressive syntax. It runs on the Java Virtual Machine (JVM), making it compatible with Java libraries and frameworks. Its ease of use, support for closures, and built-in features for working with collections make it an excellent choice for scripting, especially in scenarios like cloud security audits that require quick iteration and manipulation of data.

### Key Features of Groovy

**Dynamic Typing**: Groovy's dynamic typing allows developers to write less boilerplate code, making scripts easier to read and maintain.

**Closures**: The ability to define anonymous functions enables flexible data manipulation and event handling.

**Java Compatibility**: Groovy can seamlessly integrate with Java libraries, making it easy to utilize existing codebases.

**Scripting Capabilities**: Groovy's straightforward syntax and built-in methods simplify tasks like file manipulation, network communication, and JSON handling—all crucial for security auditing.

## 2. Setting Up Your Environment

Before diving into writing Groovy scripts for cloud security audits, you'll need to set up your development environment. Follow these steps:

**Install Java**: Ensure you have the Java Development Kit (JDK) installed, as Groovy runs on the JVM. You can download it from the official Oracle website or use OpenJDK.

**Install Groovy**: You can download Groovy from the Groovy website. Installation is straightforward, and you can verify it by running `groovy -version` in your terminal.

**IDE Support**: While you can write Groovy scripts in any text editor, using an Integrated Development Environment (IDE) like IntelliJ IDEA or Eclipse with Groovy support can enhance your productivity by providing syntax highlighting, code completion, and debugging capabilities.

## 3. Writing a Basic Groovy Script for Cloud Security Audit

Let's kick things off with a simple Groovy script that checks for open ports on a set of cloud virtual machines (VMs). This is a common security audit practice, as open ports can be gateways for malicious attacks.

### Example: Checking Open Ports

```groovy
import groovy.json.JsonSlurper import java.net.Socket

// Example of a cloud VM list def vmList = [

[name: 'VM1', ip: '192.168.1.1'],

[name: 'VM2', ip: '192.168.1.2'],

[name: 'VM3', ip: '192.168.1.3']

]

// Ports to check

def portsToCheck = [22, 80, 443, 8080]

// Function to check if a port is open def isPortOpen(ip,
```

```
port) {
try {
new Socket(ip, port).withCloseable { socket -> true }
} catch (IOException e) { return false
}
}
// Audit each VM vmList.each { vm ->
portsToCheck.each { port ->
if (isPortOpen(vm.ip, port)) {
println "${vm.name} (${vm.ip}) has port ${port} open."
} else {
println "${vm.name} (${vm.ip}) does not have port ${port} open."
}
}
}
```
```

### Script Explanation

The script defines a list of VMs, each with a name and an IP address.

It specifies which ports to check for openness.

The `isPortOpen` function attempts to create a socket connection to the specified IP and port, returning

`true` if successful (the port is open) or `false` if an
```

exception is thrown.

Finally, the script iterates over each VM and checks the defined ports, outputting the results. ## 4. Advanced Groovy Scripting Techniques for Security Audits

Once you are comfortable with basic scripting, you can explore advanced techniques to strengthen your cloud security audits.

### 4.1. Integrating with Cloud APIs

Using cloud provider APIs is essential for gathering security data programmatically. For instance, you can use AWS SDK for Groovy to fetch security group settings, IAM policies, and log data.

### Example: Fetching Security Groups in AWS

```groovy
@Grab('com.amazonaws:aws-java-sdk-ec2:1.12.0')

import com.amazonaws.services.ec2.AmazonEC2ClientBuilder

import com.amazonaws.services.ec2.model.DescribeSecurityGroupsRequest

def ec2Client = AmazonEC2ClientBuilder.defaultClient()

def response = ec2Client.describeSecurityGroups(new DescribeSecurityGroupsRequest())

response.securityGroups.each { group ->

println "Security Group: ${group.groupName} - Description: ${group.description}"
}
```

```
```

### 4.2. Parsing and Analyzing Logs

Cloud environments generate vast amounts of logs. Groovy's excellent support for JSON and XML parsing can be used to analyze log files for suspicious activities or compliance checks.

```groovy
import groovy.json.JsonSlurper

def logFile = new File('cloud_logs.json') def logs = new JsonSlurper().parse(logFile)

logs.each { logEntry ->

if (logEntry.type == 'ERROR') {

println "Error found in log: ${logEntry.message} at ${logEntry.timestamp}"

}

}
```

### 4.3. Scheduling Regular Audits

To maintain ongoing cloud security, consider using Groovy scripts in conjunction with a task scheduler or CI/CD pipeline, automating regular audits on deployment or at defined intervals.

## 5. Best Practices for Groovy Scripting in Security Audits

**Modularization**: Organize your scripts into reusable functions or classes. This enhances readability and maintainability.

**Error Handling**: Implement proper error handling to avoid crashes during execution. Use try-catch blocks judiciously.

**Documentation**: Comment your code adequately and maintain documentation for your scripts to assist future audits.

**Version Control**: Use version control systems (e.g., Git) to track changes, enabling collaboration and rollback capabilities.

**Testing**: Regularly test scripts in a controlled environment to ensure they function as expected before deploying them in production environments.

By leveraging Groovy's strengths—its simplicity, integration capabilities, and robust libraries—you can automate tedious tasks and gather valuable insights into your cloud environment's security landscape. Start small, build your skills, and soon you'll be able to create complex scripts that not only improve security but also demonstrate proactive measures in safeguarding cloud resources.

## Automating Compliance Checks and Policies

Compliance can encompass a wide range of areas, including data privacy (GDPR, HIPAA), security standards (ISO 27001, NIST), and industry-specific regulations (PCI-DSS for payment systems).

Automating compliance checks not only enhances

efficiency but also reduces the risk of human error.

In this chapter, we will explore the use of Groovy, a powerful scripting language that runs on the Java platform, for automating compliance checks and policies. Groovy's concise syntax, seamless integration with Java, and rich ecosystem make it an excellent choice for automating complex tasks within the software development lifecycle.

## Understanding Compliance Checks

Compliance checks are processes used to verify that a system adheres to predetermined standards and regulations. These checks can be manual or automated. Automated compliance checks bring several benefits:

**Consistency**: Automated environments execute checks uniformly, reducing variations caused by human error.

**Speed**: Automation can significantly reduce the time taken to complete compliance assessments.

**Scalability**: As systems grow, automated checks can scale with minimal additional resource requirements.

**Audit Trails**: Automated checks can generate logs that serve as auditable records of compliance efforts.

### Types of Compliance Checks

**Static Code Analysis**: Verifying compliance with coding standards and best practices before deployment.

**Security Scans**: Ensuring that applications do not expose vulnerabilities or security flaws.

**Configuration Management**: Confirming that system configurations comply with security baselines.

**Data Privacy Audits**: Reviewing data handling practices to ensure compliance with privacy laws. ## Setting Up the Environment

Before diving into automation with Groovy, it's essential to set up the development environment. Here's a step-by-step guide:

**Install Groovy**: Download and install Groovy from the official website or use a package manager like SDKMAN or Homebrew for macOS.

**Set Up IDE**: Use an IDE like IntelliJ IDEA or Eclipse with Groovy plugins for code completion and debugging features.

**Integrate with Jenkins (optional)**: For continuous integration (CI), setting up Jenkins can help automate the execution of compliance checks as part of your build pipeline.

**Dependencies**: Use Gradle or Maven for managing dependencies. Libraries like CheckStyle, PMD, and OWASP Dependency-Check can be helpful for compliance.

```groovy
// Example of a Gradle build file with CheckStyle dependency

plugins {
id 'groovy'
}
repositories { mavenCentral()
```

```
}
dependencies {
implementation     'org.codehaus.groovy:groovy-all:3.0.9'
checkstyle 'com.puppycrawl.tools:checkstyle:8.45'
}
```
```

## Implementing Automated Compliance Checks

### Example 1: Static Code Analysis with CheckStyle

One common automated compliance check is enforcing coding standards using CheckStyle. Below is a Groovy script that implements CheckStyle and evaluates the codebase.

```groovy
import org.gradle.api.Project

import com.puppycrawl.tools.checkstyle.CheckstylePlugin
apply plugin: CheckstylePlugin

// Configure CheckStyle settings checkstyle {

toolVersion = '8.45'

configFile = file('./config/checkstyle/checkstyle.xml')

}

// Define a task to run CheckStyle task checkCodeStyle {

doLast {

println "Running CheckStyle..." checkstyleMain.execute()

if
(checkstyleMain.getReports().get('check').getFile().exists(
```
```

```
)) { println "CheckStyle report generated. Check the
reports directory."
}
}
}

// Run CheckStyle as part of the verification phase
check.dependsOn checkCodeStyle
```
` ` `

### Example 2: Vulnerability Scanning with OWASP Dependency-Check

Another crucial compliance measure involves ensuring the software's dependencies are free from known vulnerabilities. The OWASP Dependency-Check tool helps automate this process.

```groovy
` ` `groovy plugins {
id 'org.owasp.dependencycheck' version '7.1.0'
}
// Configure Dependency Check dependencyCheck {
failBuildOnCVSS = 7.0
suppressionFile                                    =
file('./config/dependencycheck/suppressions.xml')
}
// Define a task for running Dependency-Check task
runDependencyCheck {
doLast {
```

```groovy
    println       "Running       Dependency       Check..."
    dependencyCheckAnalyze.execute()

    println "Dependency Check report generated."
  }
}

// Integrate with CI/CD pipeline check.dependsOn
runDependencyCheck
```

## Reporting and Log Generation

One of the most vital aspects of compliance automation is generating actionable reports. Groovy's ability to manipulate files and work with various data formats allows for easy reporting.

### Generate Report on Check Results

```groovy
import java.nio.file.Files import java.nio.file.Paths

def reportPath = 'build/reports/compliance-report.txt' def complianceResults = []

// Collect results from check tasks

complianceResults.add("Code       Style       Check:
${checkCodeStyle.getState()}")
complianceResults.add("Dependency       Check:
${runDependencyCheck.getState()}")

//       Create       and       write       report
Files.write(Paths.get(reportPath),       complianceResults)
println "Compliance report generated at ${reportPath}"
```

```
```

## Continuous Compliance

As modern development practices lean towards agile methodologies, it's important to integrate compliance checks continuously. Configuring Jenkins or other CI/CD tools to run compliance checks automatically at various stages, such as on pull requests, can help ensure continuous compliance.

```groovy
// Jenkinsfile example pipeline {
agent any stages {
stage('Build') { steps {
sh 'gradle build'
}
}
stage('Compliance Checks') { steps {
sh 'gradle check'
}
}
stage('Deploy') { steps {
sh 'gradle deploy'
}
}
}
```

```
}
```
```
```

Automating compliance checks and policies using Groovy not only streamlines the process, but also establishes a culture of quality and transparency in software development. By leveraging Groovy's capabilities along with existing tools and libraries, organizations can effectively monitor compliance, reduce risks, and ensure that their software aligns with regulatory standards.

# Chapter 7: Static Code Analysis with Groovy

In this chapter, we will explore how static code analysis can be effectively performed using Groovy, a dynamic language that runs on the Java platform.

### 7.1 Understanding Static Code Analysis

Static code analysis involves the use of automated tools to inspect source code for potential errors, bugs, and other quality issues before the code is compiled or tested. It can reveal problems such as:

Syntax errors

Code style violations

Potential bugs and vulnerabilities

Unused variables, methods, and classes

Complexity metrics for maintainability

The primary advantage of static code analysis is catching issues early in the development process, thereby reducing the cost and effort of fixing bugs later on.

### 7.2 Groovy: A Brief Overview

Groovy is a powerful scripting language that integrates seamlessly with Java. It brings many features and enhancements that facilitate rapid development, including:

A concise and expressive syntax

Dynamic typing

Language features such as closures, dynamic method

invocation, and operator overloading

These features make Groovy an ideal choice for rapid prototyping, domain-specific languages, and even complete application development.

### 7.3 Tools for Static Code Analysis in Groovy

When working with Groovy, several tools can assist in the static code analysis process:

**CodeNarc**:

CodeNarc is the most widely used static analysis tool for Groovy projects. It provides a set of built-in rules that check for common issues in Groovy code. CodeNarc can be integrated into your build process or run as a standalone tool.

**Example Usage**:

```groovy
apply plugin: 'codenarc'

codenarc { toolVersion = '1.5'
configFile = file('codenarc.groovy')
}
```

**PMD**:

PMD is a source code analyzer that finds common programming flaws such as unused variables, empty catch blocks, and unnecessary object creation. PMD can be configured to analyze Groovy code, leveraging its

104

comprehensive ruleset.

**Example Usage**:

```groovy
apply plugin: 'pmd'
pmd {
toolVersion = '6.0.0'
ruleSets = ['groovy-basic', 'groovy-design']
}
```

**FindBugs (SpotBugs)**:

A tool that uses static analysis to look for bugs in Java code, SpotBugs can also analyze Groovy code. By identifying potential bugs, it helps enhance the overall quality of the application.

### 7.4 Writing Custom Rules

While built-in tools like CodeNarc and PMD come with a wealth of predefined rules, sometimes you may need to enforce specific coding guidelines that are unique to your project. In Groovy, writing custom rules for CodeNarc is straightforward.

Here's a simple example of a custom rule that checks for methods with more than three parameters.

```groovy
import org.codenarc.rule.AbstractAstVisitorRule

class MaxThreeParametersRule extends
AbstractAstVisitorRule { String name =
```

```
'MaxThreeParameters'
int priority = 2
@Override
void visitMethod(MethodNode methodNode) { if
(methodNode.parameters.size() > 3) {
addViolation(methodNode, [methodNode.name])
}
}
}
```
```

To apply this rule, you would add it to your CodeNarc configuration and specify the custom rule in the

`codenarc.groovy` file.

### 7.5 Integrating Static Analysis into Development Workflow

Integrating static code analysis into your development workflow is crucial for maximizing its benefits. The recommended best practices include:

**Continuous Integration**: Incorporate static analysis checks into your CI/CD pipeline to ensure that new code follows standards before it's merged into the main branch.


*Code Reviews**: Utilize static analysis results in code reviews to highlight potential issues and facilitate discussions about coding practices among team members.

**Regular Scans**: Schedule regular scans of the codebase
```

to catch any gradually accumulating issues that could affect the project in the long run.

**Developer Training**: Provide training for developers on the tools being used and the importance of adhering to coding standards and practices recommended by static analysis.

By leveraging tools such as CodeNarc and PMD, along with the capability to define custom rules, developers can significantly improve the quality and maintainability of their code. This chapter has outlined the methodologies, best practices, and tools necessary to implement effective static code analysis in Groovy. Embracing these practices will ultimately lead to cleaner code, fewer bugs, and a smoother development process.

# Building Custom Linters and Static Analysis Tools

Groovy, an agile and dynamic language for the Java platform, provides a flexible environment for developing such tools. This chapter delves into the process of building custom linters and static analysis tools using Groovy, providing insights into its syntax, libraries, and best practices.

## Understanding Linters and Static Analysis ### What is a Linter?

A linter is a static analysis tool that analyzes source code to flag programming errors, bugs, stylistic errors, and suspicious constructs. Linters help developers adhere to coding standards and improve code quality and readability.

### What is Static Analysis?

Static analysis involves examining source code without executing it. This process can help identify potential issues such as:

**Code Smells**: Indicators of deeper problems in code structure.

**Unused Variables/Imports**: Helping clean up the codebase.

**Complexity Metrics**: Assessing the maintainability of the code.

**Potential Bugs**: Uncovering scenarios that could lead to exceptions or failures. ## Setting Up Your Environment

Before diving into code, ensure you have the requisite tools installed:

**Groovy**: Install Groovy from [Apache Groovy's website](http://groovy-lang.org/download.html).

**IDE**: Choose an IDE that supports Groovy, such as IntelliJ IDEA or Eclipse with the Groovy plugin.

**Dependencies**: Set up a `build.gradle` file if you're using Gradle for dependency management.

```groovy
```groovy plugins {

id 'groovy'

}

repositories { mavenCentral()

}

dependencies {

implementation 'org.codehaus.groovy:groovy-all:3.0.9'
```
```

```
}
```
```

## Creating a Basic Linter

Let's create a simple linter that checks for the presence of magic numbers in the code. Magic numbers are hardcoded constants in the code which can lead to maintenance difficulties.

### Step 1: Parsing the Code

The first step is to read and parse the Groovy source files. We can use Groovy's built-in capabilities to read files.

```groovy
def readSourceFile(String filePath) { new File(filePath).text
}
```

### Step 2: Identifying Magic Numbers

Next, we will write logic to identify magic numbers. A magic number is defined as any numeric value that isn't assigned to a meaningful variable.

```groovy
def findMagicNumbers(String code) { def pattern = /\b\d+\b/
def matches = code =~ pattern return matches.collect { it[0] }
}
```
```

```
```

### Step 3: Reporting Issues

After identifying magic numbers, we need to report them in a user-friendly way. This could be done via console output or even by writing to a file.

```groovy
def reportIssues(List magicNumbers) { if (magicNumbers)
{

println "Found magic numbers: ${magicNumbers.join(',
')}"

} else {

println "No magic numbers found."

}

}
```

### Step 4: Putting It All Together

Now we combine all these components into a simple linter application.

```groovy
def linter(String filePath) {

def code = readSourceFile(filePath)

def    magicNumbers    =    findMagicNumbers(code)
reportIssues(magicNumbers)

}

// Run the linter on a specified file
```

```
linter('src/main/groovy/SampleGroovyFile.groovy')
```
```

## Enhancing the Linter

Once the basic linter is up and running, you can add more features to improve its capabilities: ### Adding Rule Configuration

Create a configuration file where users can specify which rules to apply. This could be a simple JSON or YAML file.

```json
{

"rules": { "magicNumbers": true, "unusedImports": true

}

}
```

### Integrating with Other Tools

Consider integrating your linter with build tools like Gradle or Maven. By doing so, you can enforce linting as a part of the build process.

## Building Static Analysis Tools

Static analysis tools can be built using similar principles, but they often require more sophisticated parsing of the code. Groovy's Parboiled or ANTLR can be useful in these cases.

### Using Groovy's AST Transformations

Groovy supports Abstract Syntax Tree (AST)
```

transformations which allow you to analyze and manipulate code at a deeper level. You can create custom AST transformations to identify patterns, violations, and more.

### Example: Detecting Duplicate Method Definitions

You can define an AST transformation that checks for duplicate method names within a class or similar classes, significantly enhancing code quality.

```groovy
```groovy @CompileStatic

class MethodDuplicationAST {

// Implement AST transformation logic

}
```

### Creating a Plugin

For distribution, consider wrapping your linter or static analysis tool as a plugin, making it available for broader use in various environments.

By leveraging the powerful features of Groovy, developers can craft tools tailored to their specific needs, enforcing coding standards and identifying potential issues effortlessly. As the landscape of software development continues to evolve, the demand for high-quality code remains constant, making the creation of such tools an essential skill for developers.
```

# Automating Security Code Reviews

With the rise of cyber threats and vulnerabilities, it is imperative for developers to adopt practices that ensure the integrity and safety of the code they produce. Groovy, a dynamic language built on the Java platform, offers a flexible syntax and powerful features that facilitate both rapid development and robustness. This chapter delves into the automation of security code reviews in Groovy, examining techniques, best practices, and tools that can help streamline the security validation process.

## The Importance of Security Code Reviews

Security code reviews are essential for identifying vulnerabilities before they can be exploited. They help teams to:

**Identify Vulnerabilities Early**: Automating code review processes enables teams to catch potential security issues before they make their way into production.

**Educate Developers**: Ongoing reviews educate developers on secure coding practices, ultimately fostering a culture of security within the organization.

**Reduce Costs**: The cost of fixing vulnerabilities increases exponentially the further along the software development lifecycle a project progresses. Early identification significantly reduces these costs.

**Regulatory Compliance**: Many industries require compliance with security standards. Regular automated reviews help ensure adherence to these regulations.

## Setting Up the Environment

To automate security code reviews in Groovy, a few tools

and libraries can be set up to facilitate integration with existing development and CI/CD pipelines. Here's what you'll need:

**Groovy Development Environment**: Ensure you have a Groovy-compatible environment, including the Groovy SDK and build tools like Gradle or Maven.

**Static Code Analysis Tools**: Several tools can analyze Groovy code for security vulnerabilities. Some popular choices include:

**OWASP Dependency-Check**: Identifies project dependencies that may have known vulnerabilities.

**SonarQube**: Monitors code quality and provides security reports.

**PMD**: A source code analyzer that detects common programming flaws found in Java code, which can also be applied to Groovy.

**CI/CD Integration**: Incorporating security checks into the Continuous Integration and Continuous Deployment (CI/CD) pipeline ensures that security reviews are consistently performed. Popular CI/CD tools include Jenkins, GitLab CI, and GitHub Actions.

## Automating Security Code Reviews

### 1. Integrating Static Code Analysis Tools

Integrate static code analysis tools into your build pipeline. For instance, adding OWASP Dependency-Check to your Gradle build script is straightforward. Here's a sample configuration:

```groovy
plugins {
id 'org.owasp.dependencycheck' version '7.0.4'

}
dependencyCheck {
failBuildOnCVSS = 7 // Fail the build if vulnerability with
CVSS > 7 is found suppressionFile = 'dependency-check-
suppressions.xml'
format = 'ALL'
}
```

This configuration will run dependency checks during each build and enforce security standards based on CVSS scores.

### 2. Configuring SonarQube for Groovy

SonarQube can be set up to monitor your Groovy code base. To connect a Groovy project with SonarQube, include the following in your `build.gradle`:

```groovy
plugins {
id 'org.sonarqube' version '3.3'
} .
sonarqube { properties {
property "sonar.projectKey", "your_project_key" property
"sonar.host.url", "http://localhost:9000" property
"sonar.login", "your_sonar_token" property
"sonar.language", "groovy"
```

property "sonar.sourceEncoding", "UTF-8"

}

}

```
` ` `
```

Running `gradle sonarqube` will push your code to SonarQube, allowing you to analyze it for potential vulnerabilities.

### 3. Setting Up PMD for Code Analysis

PMD can also be employed for more granular code analysis. Integrate PMD in your build script as follows:

```groovy
apply plugin: 'pmd'

pmd {

toolVersion = '6.36.0'

ruleSets = ['java-basic', 'groovy-basic'] // Include Groovy rules

}

tasks.withType(Pmd) { reports {

xml.enabled false

html.enabled true // Generate HTML reports

}

}
```

When you run your build, PMD will evaluate the code against the rules specified and provide reports outlining any detected issues.

### 4. Automating in CI/CD

To fully leverage automation, include the analysis tasks in your CI/CD pipeline configuration. For example, in a Jenkins pipeline, you might include the following stages:

```groovy
groovy pipeline {

agent any stages {

stage('Build') { steps {

sh './gradlew clean build'

}

}

stage('Static Analysis') { steps {

sh './gradlew dependencyCheckAnalyze sonarqube pmd'

}

}

stage('Test') { steps {

sh './gradlew test'

}

}

}

post {

always {

archiveArtifacts artifacts: '**/build/libs/*.jar' junit '**/build/test-results/**/*.xml' waitUntil {
```

```
script {
// Wait for SonarQube analysis to be completed return
checkSonarQubeStatus()
}
}
}
}
}
```
```

This pipeline ensures that every build triggers a security analysis.

By integrating tools such as OWASP Dependency-Check, SonarQube, and PMD into CI/CD pipelines, teams can address vulnerabilities proactively. Embracing these practices ensures that applications not only meet functionality requirements but also adhere to stringent security standards, ultimately leading to more robust and resilient software.
```

# Chapter 8: Dynamic Application Security Testing (DAST)

DAST tools simulate attacks on a running application to identify vulnerabilities without inspecting the underlying code. This chapter will explore DAST, focusing on how it can be leveraged in Groovy applications, the language widely used in the Groovy ecosystem, particularly with web applications built on frameworks like Grails and Spring Boot.

## 8.1 Understanding DAST

Before diving into DAST in Groovy, it's essential to grasp what DAST entails. DAST tools operate by interacting with an application in real-time, mimicking the actions of a potential attacker. They can assess various application layers, including the front-end UI, APIs, and database servers, thereby uncovering vulnerabilities such as:

Cross-Site Scripting (XSS)

SQL Injection

Cross-Site Request Forgery (CSRF)

Insecure Direct Object References (IDOR)

DAST is particularly valuable as it does not require access to the source code, making it ideal for security assessments of third-party applications or those where developers are not familiar with code-level vulnerabilities.

## 8.2 Why Use DAST with Groovy?

Groovy, a powerful, agile language for the Java platform, is known for its ease of use and expressiveness, making it a popular choice for developers. It is especially prevalent in applications developed with the Grails framework. The nature of web applications created with Groovy facilitates DAST, as these applications tend to expose rich user interfaces and APIs.

Using DAST with Groovy applications allows developers to:

**Identify vulnerabilities early**: By implementing DAST in the application lifecycle, vulnerabilities can be identified before they reach production.

**Enhance application resilience**: By continuously testing applications, organizations can improve their security posture and respond quickly to emerging threats.

**Compliance with standards**: Many regulatory standards require dynamic testing, and using DAST helps maintain compliance.

## 8.3 Integrating DAST into Groovy Applications

Integrating DAST into Groovy applications can be accomplished with various commercial and open-source DAST tools available in the market. Some notable tools include:

**OWASP ZAP (Zed Attack Proxy)**: An open-source DAST tool that provides automated scanners and various testing tools to find vulnerabilities in web applications.

**Burp Suite**: A popular tool for web application security testing that offers robust scanning and manual testing capabilities.

**Acunetix**: A commercial tool that automates the scanning of web applications, providing a detailed report on identified vulnerabilities.

### 8.3.1 Setting Up OWASP ZAP with a Groovy Application

In this section, we will discuss how to set up OWASP ZAP with a Groovy application. ### Step 1: Install OWASP ZAP

Download and install OWASP ZAP from the official OWASP website. It is available for multiple platforms including Windows, macOS, and Linux.

### Step 2: Run Your Groovy Application

Ensure your Groovy application (for example, a Grails app) is running locally, typically on

`http://localhost:8080`.

### Step 3: Configure ZAP to Proxy Your Application

Open OWASP ZAP.

Go to Tools > Options > Local proxy and ensure that the port (default is 8080) is set to match your application's server.

Configure your browser to use OWASP ZAP as a proxy. You can usually find this option within your browser's network settings.

### Step 4: Start Scanning

With the application running and ZAP configured, you can start scanning:

In ZAP, click on the "Quick Start" tab.

Select "Automated Scan."

Enter the URL of your Groovy application and click "Attack."

ZAP will begin crawling and scanning your application for common vulnerabilities. Review the results tab to view identified issues categorized by severity.

## 8.4 Analyzing DAST Results

The output from DAST tools requires careful analysis. ZAP, for instance, provides:

**Alerts**: A breakdown of recognized vulnerabilities with descriptions and remediation guidance.

**Site Map**: A visual representation of the application's structure, including identified endpoints and how they were discovered.

When reviewing DAST results:

Assess the criticality of vulnerabilities: Focus your efforts on high- and medium-severity issues first.

Provide remediation recommendations: Include actionable steps to fix identified vulnerabilities, such as input validation and output encoding for XSS issues.

Incorporate findings into the development workflow: Communicate findings to developers and integrate them into issue tracking systems to ensure timely resolution.

## 8.5 Best Practices for DAST in Groovy Applications

To maximize the effectiveness of DAST in Groovy applications, consider the following best practices:

**Regular Scanning**: Implement regular scans in your

CI/CD pipeline to catch vulnerabilities as soon as they are introduced.

**Combine with Other Testing Methods**: Use DAST in conjunction with Static Application Security Testing (SAST) to cover both code and running application vulnerabilities.

**Educate Development Teams**: Ensure that your development teams understand the vulnerabilities detected by DAST tools and how to mitigate them.

**Keep Tools Updated**: Regularly update your DAST tools to utilize the latest vulnerability signatures and scanning capabilities.

By integrating DAST into the development lifecycle and leveraging tools like OWASP ZAP, developers can proactively address security concerns, ensuring the robustness and resilience of their applications. As web security threats continue to evolve, so must the strategies we employ to defend against them, making DAST an indispensable part of any modern software development practice.

## Creating Groovy Scripts for Penetration Testing

Penetration testing, a simulated cyber attack aimed at evaluating the security posture of an organization, has emerged as a fundamental practice in this domain. Creating scripts to automate and streamline this process can significantly enhance the efficiency and effectiveness of penetration tests. This chapter aims to explore the creation of Groovy scripts tailored for penetration testing, discussing the language's features, libraries, and best practices.

## What is Groovy?

Groovy is an agile and versatile programming language that runs on the Java Virtual Machine (JVM). With a syntax similar to Java, Groovy enhances developers' productivity through its dynamic features, concise scripts, and rich ecosystem of libraries. Its ability to integrate seamlessly with Java makes it a powerful tool for penetration testers who wish to leverage existing Java resources while benefiting from Groovy's expressiveness.

### Advantages of Using Groovy for Penetration Testing

**Simplicity**: Groovy's syntax is simpler and more concise than Java's, allowing for quicker script writing and easier readability.

**Integration**: As a JVM language, Groovy can seamlessly use Java libraries, offering penetration testers access to a wealth of resources.

**Dynamic Nature**: The dynamic capabilities of Groovy facilitate runtime changes, making it ideal for scripting tasks tied to iterative testing.

**Quick Prototyping**: Groovy facilitates rapid development cycles, allowing testers to quickly prototype and test strategies without a lengthy setup process.

## Setting Up the Environment

Before diving into script creation, setting up the Groovy development environment is essential. Below are simple steps to get started:

**Install Java Development Kit (JDK)**: Download and install the JDK if you haven't already. Groovy is based on

124

Java, so it is a prerequisite.

**Download Groovy**: Visit the official Groovy website to download the latest version. Alternatively, use a package manager like `Homebrew` or `SDKMAN` to install Groovy seamlessly.

**Set Environment Variables**: Ensure that the Groovy installation path is correctly set in your system's environment variables to run Groovy commands from the shell or command prompt.

## Understanding Groovy Syntax and Features

Familiarizing yourself with Groovy's core syntax and features can significantly streamline your scripting process. Key components include:

- **Variables**: Groovy allows dynamic typing. You can declare variables using the `def` keyword:

```groovy
def ipAddress = '192.168.1.1'
```


- **Control Structures**: Groovy supports common constructs like loops and conditionals. A simple `if-else` statement:


```groovy
if (statusCode == 200) { println "Success"
} else {
```

```groovy
println "Failure"
}
```

- **Collections**: Collections in Groovy, such as lists and maps, are easy to manipulate:

```groovy
def ports = [22, 80, 443] ports.each { port ->
println "Scanning port: $port"
}
```

## Writing Groovy Scripts for Common Penetration Testing Tasks

To illustrate Groovy's application within penetration testing, we'll explore common tasks such as network scanning, service enumeration, and exploiting vulnerabilities.

### 1. Network Scanning

A basic network scanner script can be built using Groovy's socket capabilities. The following example scans a specified IP address for open ports:

```groovy
import java.net.SocketTimeoutException

def scanPorts(String ip, int startPort, int endPort) { for (int port = startPort; port <= endPort; port++) {
try {
```

```groovy
Socket socket = new Socket()
socket.connect(new InetSocketAddress(ip, port), 1000) // 1-second timeout println "Port $port is open"
socket.close()
} catch (SocketTimeoutException e) {
// Port is closed
} catch (IOException e) { println "Error: ${e.message}"
}
}
}
def targetIP = '192.168.1.1' scanPorts(targetIP, 1, 1024)
```

### 2. Service Enumeration

Once open ports are found, enumerating services running on those ports can provide valuable insights. Groovy can invoke external scripts—such as `nmap`—using the `ProcessBuilder` class.

```groovy
def nmapScan(String ip) {
def process = new ProcessBuilder("nmap", "-sV", ip).start() process.inputStream.eachLine { line ->
println line
}
process.waitFor()
```

```
}
nmapScan(targetIP)
```

### 3. Exploiting Vulnerabilities

Scripting common exploitation techniques can also be performed in Groovy. For example, let's create a simple script to perform SQL injection testing against a vulnerable webpage.

```groovy
import groovy.json.JsonSlurper import groovyx.net.http.RESTClient

def testSQLInjection(String url) { def client = new RESTClient(url)

def sqlPayloads = ["' OR '1'='1", "'; DROP TABLE users;--"]

sqlPayloads.each { payload ->

def response = client.get(path: "", query: [username: payload]) if (response.status == 200) {

println "Potential SQL Injection found with payload: $payload"
}
}
}
testSQLInjection("http://vulnerable.app/login")
```

128

## Best Practices for Groovy Scripting

**Modularity**: Organize scripts into reusable functions and classes to promote code reusability and clarity.

**Error Handling**: Implement comprehensive error handling to gracefully manage unexpected scenarios during execution.

**Documentation**: Comment your code and create documentation to maintain clarity and facilitate future enhancements or collaborations.

**Security Considerations**: Ensure that sensitive information (e.g., passwords, API keys) is handled securely and not hard-coded into scripts.

By mastering Groovy, cybersecurity professionals can develop robust scripts tailored to their specific needs and responses to an ever-evolving threat landscape. As you implement the techniques discussed, remember that proactive and adaptive measures are essential in the ongoing challenge of securing systems against malicious attacks.

## Automating DAST in DevSecOps Pipelines

DevSecOps emphasizes incorporating security practices within the DevOps pipeline, ensuring that security measures are baked into applications from the start. One of the critical components of ensuring the security of web applications is Dynamic Application Security Testing (DAST). This chapter will explore how to automate DAST within DevSecOps pipelines using Groovy, a versatile scripting language that runs on the Java platform.

## Understanding DAST

Dynamic Application Security Testing is a black-box testing method used to identify vulnerabilities by executing the application and evaluating its behavior. Unlike static analysis, which examines source code, DAST analyzes the running application, enabling it to detect runtime vulnerabilities, misconfigurations, and issues introduced through user interactions.

### Benefits of Automating DAST

**Early Detection**: By incorporating DAST in CI/CD pipelines, vulnerabilities can be detected while developers are still active in the code, making them easier to rectify.

**Continuous Monitoring**: Automated testing allows for continuous assessment of applications, especially as they undergo frequent changes.

**Reduced Costs**: Finding and fixing vulnerabilities during development is significantly cheaper than addressing them after deployment.

**Integration with Existing Tools**: Automating DAST can facilitate seamless integration with existing CI/CD tools, enhancing the overall security posture.

## Groovy: A Powerful Tool for Automation

Groovy is an object-oriented programming language that integrates seamlessly with Java, making it an ideal choice for scripting within DevSecOps environments. Its concise syntax and ability to handle complex tasks with ease allow developers to automate processes without extensive overhead. When it comes to DAST automation, Groovy can be utilized in multiple ways, including scripting, job or pipeline definitions in Jenkins, and integrating tools such as OWASP ZAP.

## Setting Up the DAST Environment

Before automating DAST within a CI/CD pipeline, ensure you have the following set up:

**Groovy Environment**: Ensure Groovy is installed and available in your environment.

**CI/CD Tool**: For our examples, we will focus on Jenkins as a widely used CI/CD platform.

**DAST Tool**: Install and configure OWASP ZAP (Zed Attack Proxy), which provides an API for automated interactions.

### Installing OWASP ZAP

You can install OWASP ZAP via Docker or directly on your machine. For Docker, the command is straightforward:

```bash
docker pull owasp/zap2docker-stable
```

Once installed, you can run ZAP in daemon mode, which allows scripts to interact with the tool:

```bash
docker run -d -p 8080:8080 owasp/zap2docker-stable zap.sh -daemon -host 0.0.0.0 -port 8080 -config api.disablekey=true
```

## Integrating DAST with Jenkins using Groovy ###

Creating a Jenkins Pipeline

To automate DAST using Groovy in Jenkins, follow these steps:

**Create a New Pipeline Job**: In Jenkins, create a new item and select "Pipeline."

**Configure the Pipeline Script**: Use Groovy to define your pipeline. Here's a sample script:

```groovy
groovy pipeline {

agent any

stages {

stage('Build') { steps {

// Example build step

echo 'Building the application...' sh 'mvn clean package'

}

}

stage('Deploy') { steps {

// Deploy the application (to a test environment) echo 'Deploying the application...'

sh 'docker-compose up -d'

}

}

stage('Run DAST') { steps {

script {

// Call OWASP ZAP to perform dynamic testing echo 'Running DAST with OWASP ZAP...'
```

```
def zapUrl = "http://localhost:8080" def targetUrl =
"http://yourapp.test"
// Start the scan
sh              "curl          -X          POST
\"${zapUrl}/JSON/ascan/action/scan/?url=${targetUrl}\"
"


// Wait for the scan to complete sleep(time: 30, unit:
'SECONDS')


// Retrieve the results
def alertResults = sh(script: "curl -X GET
\"${zapUrl}/JSON/core/view/alerts/?baseurl=${targetUrl
}&start=0&count=100\"",


returnStdout: true) echo alertResults
}
}
}
stage('Cleanup') { steps {
echo 'Cleaning up...'
// Stop and remove the Docker containers sh 'docker-
compose down'
}
}
```

```
}
}
```
```
` ` `
```

### Explanation of the Pipeline Script

**Stages**: The pipeline is divided into several stages, including Build, Deploy, Run DAST, and Cleanup.

**DAST Stage**: During the Run DAST stage, the script interacts with the OWASP ZAP API using `curl` commands. It starts an active scan against the target application and retrieves any alerts afterward.

**Dynamic Results Handling**: The results from the DAST scan can be processed and reported within Jenkins, either by printing them on the console or by integrating with tools like JIRA for issue tracking.

## Best Practices for DAST Automation

**Scan Regularly**: Integrate DAST scans in each cycle of your CI/CD pipeline, not just as a one-off.

**Prioritize Vulnerabilities**: Not all vulnerabilities carry the same risk. Implement logic to prioritize findings, enabling teams to rectify high-risk issues first.

**Feedback Loop**: Automate notifications or reports to developers when vulnerabilities are detected.

**Resource Management**: Ensure responsible resource allocation, as dynamic scanning can be resource-intensive.

By embedding DAST in the CI/CD workflow, organizations can maintain a strong security posture, identifying and mitigating vulnerabilities early in the development process. With the growing trend toward integrated security practices, leveraging tools like Groovy and OWASP ZAP enables teams to build applications that are not only functional but also secure by design. By adopting these practices, organizations can confidently embrace the DevSecOps transformation.

# Chapter 9: Managing Secrets and Credentials

Whether you're building applications that interface with databases, APIs, or cloud services, ensuring that sensitive information remains protected is a critical concern for developers. This chapter delves into effective strategies and practices for managing secrets in Groovy applications, exploring various tools, libraries, and techniques available for developers.

## 9.1 Understanding the Importance of Secrets Management

Secrets management refers to the processes and tools used to protect sensitive information, such as API keys, passwords, and tokens. The primary reasons behind managing secrets effectively include:

**Security**: Protecting sensitive data from unauthorized access and potential breaches is vital.

**Compliance**: Many regulations require that sensitive information be stored and managed securely.

**Operational Integrity**: Ensuring that applications function reliably and securely without exposing critical secrets.

## 9.2 Best Practices for Storing and Accessing Secrets

When working with secrets in Groovy, it is essential to adopt best practices to minimize the risk of exposure. Here are some recommendations:

### 9.2.1 Avoid Hardcoding Secrets

Hardcoding secrets directly in your source code is one of

the most significant security risks. Instead, consider alternative methods for managing secrets:

**Configuration Files**: Externalize configuration files and exclude them from version control. Use

`.gitignore` to prevent files containing secrets from being committed. ### 9.2.2 Environment Variables

Environment variables provide a secure way to manage secrets. You can access environment variables in

Groovy using:

```groovy
def secretKey = System.getenv('SECRET_KEY')
```

This approach keeps secrets out of your codebase while allowing for easy configuration across different environments.

### 9.2.3 Secure Vaults

Using secret management tools like HashiCorp Vault, AWS Secrets Manager, or Azure Key Vault can provide a comprehensive solution for managing and accessing secrets. These tools offer:

**Encryption**: Secrets are stored in an encrypted format.

**Access Control**: Fine-grained permission models ensure that only authorized entities can access specific secrets.

**Audit Trails**: Logging and auditing capabilities for tracking access and modifications to secrets.

## 9.3 Integrating Secrets Management in Groovy

Applications

Let's explore how to integrate secrets management in a Groovy application using a popular library or tool. ### 9.3.1 Using Spring Boot for Secrets Management

If you're developing your Groovy application using Spring Boot, you can leverage its built-in support for external configuration properties.

#### Step 1: Add Dependencies

Ensure you have the necessary dependencies in your `build.gradle` file:

```groovy
dependencies {

implementation 'org.springframework.boot:spring-boot-starter'

implementation 'org.springframework.boot:spring-boot-starter-configuration-processor'

}
```

#### Step 2: Configure Secrets

You can use application properties files (e.g., `application.properties` or `application.yml`) to specify your secrets:

```properties

# application.properties secret.key=your_secret_key
```

#### Step 3: Access Secrets in Groovy

You can create a component to access these secrets easily:

```groovy
import
org.springframework.beans.factory.annotation.Value
import org.springframework.stereotype.Component

@Component

class SecretService {

@Value('${secret.key}') String secretKey

String getSecretKey() { return secretKey

}

}
```

This approach allows you to inject the secret value wherever needed, promoting cleaner and more maintainable code.

## 9.4 Encrypting Secrets

Although using environment variables and secret management tools enhances security, it's crucial to encrypt sensitive data at rest and in transit. In Groovy, you can use libraries such as JCE (Java Cryptography Extension) to encrypt and decrypt secrets.

### Example: Encrypting a Secret

```groovy
import javax.crypto.Cipher

import          javax.crypto.KeyGenerator          import
javax.crypto.SecretKey

import          javax.crypto.spec.SecretKeySpec          class
```

```
EncryptionUtil {

def encrypt(String data, SecretKey secretKey) { Cipher
cipher           =           Cipher.getInstance("AES")
cipher.init(Cipher.ENCRYPT_MODE, secretKey)

return
cipher.doFinal(data.bytes).encodeBase64().toString()

}

def decrypt(String encryptedData, SecretKey secretKey) {
Cipher      cipher     =      Cipher.getInstance("AES")
cipher.init(Cipher.DECRYPT_MODE, secretKey)

return                                              new
String(cipher.doFinal(encryptedData.decodeBase64()))

}

static SecretKey generateKey() {

KeyGenerator             keyGenerator             =
KeyGenerator.getInstance("AES") keyGenerator.init(128)

return keyGenerator.generateKey()

}

}
```
` ` `

Using this `EncryptionUtil`, you can securely encrypt and
store sensitive information, ensuring that even if
unauthorized access occurs, the data remains protected.

## 9.5 Auditing and Monitoring Secrets Access

An essential aspect of managing secrets is ensuring that
access is logged and monitored. This can help identify

potential breaches or misuse. Utilize logging frameworks compatible with Groovy, such as Log4j or SLF4J, to capture access attempts, including timestamps, user identities, and the nature of requests.

### Example: Logging Access to Secrets

```groovy
import org.slf4j.Logger

import org.slf4j.LoggerFactory class SecretService {

private final Logger logger = LoggerFactory.getLogger(SecretService)

...

String getSecretKey() {

logger.info("Accessing secret key at ${new Date()}") return secretKey

}

}
```

By avoiding hardcoding secrets, utilizing environment variables, third-party secret management tools, and implementing encryption, developers can significantly enhance the security of their applications.

Furthermore, keeping audit logs of secret access will help maintain accountability and thwart potential threats. As security landscapes continue to evolve, developers must remain vigilant and adaptive to ensure the safety and integrity of sensitive information.

# Automating Secrets Management with Groovy

Secrets can include API keys, database credentials, encryption keys, and other configurations that, if mishandled or exposed, can lead to catastrophic security breaches. This chapter explores how to automate secrets management using Groovy, a powerful scripting language that integrates seamlessly with Java, enhances productivity, and simplifies complex tasks.

## 1. Understanding Secrets Management

Secrets management is the process of managing digital authentication credentials and sensitive information throughout their lifecycle. This includes:

**Creation**: Generating secrets in a secure manner.

**Storage**: Safely storing secrets so that unauthorized access is prevented.

**Access**: Granting or denying access to secrets based on user roles and permissions.

**Rotation**: Periodically changing secrets to mitigate risks.

**Audit**: Tracking access and usage of secrets for compliance and security purposes.

An effective secrets management solution must ensure confidentiality, integrity, and availability of sensitive information, all while minimizing operational overhead.

## 2. Why Groovy?

Groovy is a versatile and expressive language that runs on the Java Virtual Machine (JVM). It is recognized for its concise syntax and powerful features, which make it a great choice for scripting and automation tasks. Here are some reasons to use Groovy for secrets management:

**Integration**: Groovy can easily integrate with existing Java applications and systems, allowing developers to leverage existing libraries for security and data management.

**Ease of Use**: Groovy's simplicity makes it accessible to developers of varying expertise. Its syntax is designed for productivity, reducing the time taken to write complex scripts.

**Dynamic Nature**: Groovy allows for dynamic typing and metaprogramming, which can be useful in scenarios requiring flexibility.

## 3. Setting Up Groovy for Secrets Management

Before we can dive into automating secrets management, we need to set up the Groovy environment and choose a secrets management tool or service. Common options include HashiCorp Vault, AWS Secrets Manager, and Azure Key Vault. For illustration, we'll proceed with HashiCorp Vault, as it is open-source and widely adopted.

### 3.1 Installing Groovy

You can install Groovy by downloading it directly from the [Groovy website](https://groovy.apache.org/download.html) or by using a package manager. For example, on macOS, you can use Homebrew:

```bash
brew install groovy
```

```
```

### 3.2 Setting Up HashiCorp Vault

**Installation**: You can download and install Vault from the [HashiCorp website](https://www.hashicorp.com/products/vault).

**Initialization**: Start the Vault server in development mode for quick setup:

```bash
vault server -dev
```

**Authenticate**: Open a new terminal window to authenticate and interact with Vault:

```bash
export VAULT_ADDR='http://127.0.0.1:8200' vault login <your-development-token>
```

## 4. Writing Scripts for Secrets Management

Below is a simple Groovy script to automate the creation, retrieval, and deletion of secrets using HashiCorp Vault. The script assumes you have already set up your Vault server as mentioned above.

### 4.1 Creating Secrets

```groovy
import groovy.json.JsonSlurper        import groovy.json.JsonOutput

def vaultToken = "<your-vault-token>"
```

```groovy
def                vaultAddr                =
"http://127.0.0.1:8200/v1/secret/data/my-secret"

def secretData = [data: [username: "admin", password:
"supersecretpass"]]

// Create a new secret def createSecret() {

def json = JsonOutput.toJson(secretData)

def connection = new URL(vaultAddr).openConnection()
connection.setRequestMethod("POST")
connection.setRequestProperty("X-Vault-Token",
vaultToken)                connection.setDoOutput(true)
connection.outputStream.withWriter { it << json }


// Check response

if (connection.responseCode == 200) { println "Secret
created successfully."

} else {

println        "Failed        to        create        secret:
${connection.responseCode}"

}

}

createSecret()
```
```

### 4.2 Retrieving Secrets

```groovy
def retrieveSecret() {

def connection = new URL(vaultAddr).openConnection()
```

145
```

```groovy
connection.setRequestMethod("GET")
connection.setRequestProperty("X-Vault-Token",
vaultToken)

def jsonResponse = connection.inputStream.text

def        parsedJson        =        new
JsonSlurper().parseText(jsonResponse) def secret =
parsedJson.data

println  "Retrieved  Secret:  ${secret.username}  /
${secret.password}"
}

retrieveSecret()
```

### 4.3 Deleting Secrets

```groovy
def deleteSecret() {

def deleteAddr = "http://127.0.0.1:8200/v1/secret/my-
secret"        def        connection        =        new
URL(deleteAddr).openConnection()
connection.setRequestMethod("DELETE")
connection.setRequestProperty("X-Vault-Token",
vaultToken)

if (connection.responseCode == 204) { println "Secret
deleted successfully."

} else {

println        "Failed        to        delete        secret:
${connection.responseCode}"
```

```
        }
    }
    deleteSecret()
```
```

## 5. Best Practices for Secrets Management

While automating secrets management with Groovy can significantly enhance security and efficiency, organizations must adhere to best practices:

**Least Privilege Access**: Ensure that only authorized personnel have access to the secrets, using role- based access controls in your secrets management tool.

**Audit Logging**: Enable audit logging in your secrets management solution to track access and modifications.

**Secret Rotation**: Implement a strategy for regular rotation of secrets to reduce the risk of exposure.

**Environment Segregation**: Use different secrets for development, testing, and production environments.

By leveraging tools like HashiCorp Vault and Groovy's rich ecosystem, organizations can sow the seeds of resilience in their development workflows. The fast-paced world of agile development demands robust solutions for managing sensitive data, and Groovy provides a compelling means of achieving that goal. As we move forward, the principles and practices outlined in this chapter will serve as valuable guidelines for sustainable secrets management in modern software development.
```

# Securely Handling API Keys and Environment Variables

These pieces of information can provide access to powerful services and databases, and their exposure could lead to severe security breaches. In this chapter, we will explore the best practices for securely managing API keys and environment variables in Groovy, a versatile programming language that runs on the Java Virtual Machine (JVM).

## 1. Understanding API Keys and Environment Variables

API keys are unique identifiers used to authenticate requests associated with your application. They are often used to connect to external services and provide a mechanism for tracking and controlling how the API is being used. Similarly, environment variables are key-value pairs maintained outside of your application code that help manage configurations and secure sensitive information, such as database credentials, third-party service passwords, or secret tokens.

Storing these pieces of information in your codebase can expose them to various risks, including unintended access within your source control system, deployment pipelines, or through process dumps.

## 2. Best Practices for Storing API Keys and Environment Variables ### 2.1 Use Environment Variables

A best practice for managing sensitive data is to avoid hardcoding API keys directly into your code. Instead, leverage environment variables that can be set in your operating system or deployment environment.

#### How to Access Environment Variables in Groovy:

Groovy provides a simple way to access environment variables using the `System.getenv()` method:

```groovy
def apiKey = System.getenv("MY_API_KEY")
```

### 2.2 Utilize a Configuration File

For applications that require multiple configurations or settings, consider using a configuration file that is excluded from version control. This file can hold environment-specific variables, and you can use libraries such as Apache Commons Configuration or even Groovy's built-in `ConfigSlurper` to retrieve the values.

#### Example:

```groovy
import groovy.util.ConfigSlurper

def config = new ConfigSlurper().parse(new File('config.groovy').toURL()) def apiKey = config.apiKey
```

**Note:** Ensure that your configuration file is included in `.gitignore` to prevent it from being committed to your repository.

### 2.3 Leverage Secrets Management Tools

For complex applications or enterprise solutions, consider using dedicated secrets management tools like HashiCorp Vault, AWS Secrets Manager, or Azure Key Vault. These tools provide robust features to store, manage, and access sensitive information securely.

#### Example using AWS Secrets Manager:

You can access secrets stored in AWS Secrets Manager using the AWS SDK for Java. Here's a code snippet demonstrating how to retrieve a secret in Groovy:

```groovy
@Grab('com.amazonaws:aws-java-sdk-secretsmanager:1.11.1000')

import com.amazonaws.services.secretsmanager.AWSSecretsManagerClientBuilder import com.amazonaws.services.secretsmanager.model.GetSecretValueRequest

def secretName = "mySecretName"

def client = AWSSecretsManagerClientBuilder.standard().build()

def request = new GetSecretValueRequest().withSecretId(secretName) def response = client.getSecretValue(request)

def secret = response.secretString
```

### 2.4 Rotate API Keys Regularly

Regularly rotating your API keys minimizes the risk of key exposure. Develop an automated process to rotate keys and update the associated application settings accordingly.

## 3. Secure Access Controls ### 3.1 Limit Permissions

Ensure that the permissions associated with an API key are kept to a minimum. When generating API keys, only enable access to the necessary resources needed by your application.

### 3.2 Use Fine-Grained API Keys

If supported by the service provider, use fine-grained API keys that limit scope to specific actions or resources needed by your application.

## 4. Enhanced Security Practices ### 4.1 Encrypt Sensitive Information

While storing sensitive information in environment variables is a good practice, adding an additional layer of security by encrypting the data can further minimize risks.

### 4.2 Monitor API Usage

Implement logging and monitoring for your API usage. Many cloud providers offer analytics tools that allow you to track the use of your keys and detect anomalies.

### 4.3 Educate Your Team

Security is a shared responsibility. Educate your team about secure coding practices and the importance of protecting sensitive information.

By following best practices such as using environment variables, configuration files, secrets management tools, and regularly rotating API keys, you can significantly reduce the risk of exposing sensitive information. The integration of security measures into your development workflow will not only protect your application but also build trust with your users. Implementing these practices should be a fundamental aspect of your software development lifecycle.

# Chapter 10: Advanced Groovy for Threat Detection

In this chapter, we will delve deeper into advanced Groovy programming techniques specifically tailored for threat detection. We will cover various aspects, including pattern recognition, data analysis, integration with security tools, and real-time monitoring.

### 10.1. Understanding the Threat Landscape

Before we dive into Groovy, it's essential to understand the current threat landscape. Cybercriminals employ various sophisticated methods to breach systems, making traditional detection mechanisms often inadequate. Techniques like polymorphic malware, social engineering, and insider threats necessitate an adaptable and rapid response strategy. Groovy's ability to automate tasks, parse data, and facilitate real-time alerts makes it an ideal candidate for enhancing threat detection capabilities.

### 10.2. Groovy Basics for Security Professionals

For those new to Groovy, it's important first to grasp some fundamental concepts:

**Syntax and Semantics**: Groovy's syntax is concise and often resembles Java, which allows Java developers to transition easily. However, it incorporates more flexible programming paradigms such as closures and dynamic typing.

**Data Structures**: Groovy offers powerful data structures like lists, maps, and ranges that simplify data manipulation, which is crucial when handling threat data.

**Integration with Java Libraries**: Groovy can leverage Java libraries, making it versatile for integrating with existing security tools, frameworks, and protocols.

### 10.3. Data Aggregation and Parsing

Effective threat detection relies heavily on analyzing vast amounts of data from different sources. Groovy's capabilities allow for elegant data aggregation and parsing. Here's how you can implement these techniques:

#### 10.3.1. Parsing Logs

Logs from servers, firewalls, and intrusion detection systems are valuable for identifying threats. Use Groovy's built-in capabilities to parse and analyze log files:

```groovy
def logFile = new File("system.log") logFile.eachLine { line ->

if (line.contains("ERROR") || line.contains("FAILURE")) {
println "Alert: ${line}"

}

}
```

This simple script scans through a log file for critical entries, demonstrating Groovy's efficiency in log parsing.

#### 10.3.2. Aggregating Threat Intelligence

Security information feeds provide insights into emerging threats. Utilizing Groovy, you can aggregate and analyze data from these feeds:

```groovy
```

```groovy
def feeds = ["feed1.json", "feed2.json"] def aggregatedData
= []
```

feeds.each { feed ->

```groovy
def json = new JsonSlurper().parse(new File(feed))
aggregatedData += json
```

}

// Filter for known indicators of compromise (IoCs)

```groovy
def knownIoCs = aggregatedData.findAll { it.type ==
'malware' || it.type == 'phishing' }
```
```
```

This snippet illustrates how to aggregate and filter threat intelligence feeds with Groovy's capabilities. ### 10.4. Building Custom Detection Rules

One of the powerful features of Groovy is the ability to create custom detection rules tailored to specific environments. Here's an example of constructing a rule-based engine for monitoring suspicious activities:

```groovy
class DetectionRule { String name Closure condition

boolean evaluate(data) { return condition(data)

}
}

def rules = [

new DetectionRule(name: 'Suspicious Login', condition: {
data -> data.loginAttempts > 5 && data.ipAddress !=
'trustedIP' }),
```

```groovy
new DetectionRule(name: 'File Integrity Check',
condition: { data -> data.fileChanges.any { it.type ==
'DELETE' } })
]
def activityLog = [loginAttempts: 7, ipAddress:
'unknownIP', fileChanges: [[type: 'DELETE', file:
'config.txt']]]
rules.each { rule ->
if (rule.evaluate(activityLog)) {
println "Alert: ${rule.name} triggered!"
}
}
```

This approach allows security analysts to create custom rules, improving detection tailored to organizational needs.

### 10.5. Real-time Monitoring and Alerting

In the realm of cybersecurity, time is of the essence. Groovy's support for integration with various web frameworks allows for the development of real-time monitoring dashboards. Using Groovy's Ratpack framework, you can quickly set up a monitoring dashboard:

```groovy
import ratpack.server.RatpackServer
```

```
RatpackServer.start { server -> server.handlers { chain ->
chain.get("monitor") { ctx ->
// Simulate checking for threats
def threatsDetected = checkForThreats() ctx.render
"Threats Detected: ${threatsDetected}"
}
}
}
def checkForThreats() {
// Logic to check for existing threats return 3 // Example
of detected threats
}
```

The above snippet outlines a basic web server that listens for monitoring requests, demonstrating how Groovy can handle real-time threat detection scenarios.

### 10.6. Integrating with Existing Security Tools

Groovy's interoperability with other languages and tools enhances its value significantly. Many enterprise security solutions provide RESTful APIs, enabling Groovy scripts to interact easily. For instance, integrating with a common SIEM (Security Information and Event Management) tool can be done as follows:

```groovy
import          groovy.json.JsonOutput          import
groovy.json.JsonSlurper                          import
```

```
groovyx.net.http.RESTClient

def          client          =          new
RESTClient('https://siem.example.com/api/')          def
response = client.get(path: "/alerts")

def alerts = new JsonSlurper().parseText(response.data)
alerts.each { alert ->

println "Alert ID: ${alert.id}, Severity: ${alert.severity}"

// Further actions like logging or escalation can be
implemented here

}
```
` ` `

This example illustrates how Groovy can pull data from a SIEM tool, allowing you to act upon alerts and improve situational awareness.

The versatility of Groovy allows cybersecurity professionals to adapt the language to their specific contexts, making it an invaluable tool in the modern threat landscape. As technology continues to advance, leveraging such scripting capabilities can significantly enhance an organization's resilience against cyber threats. By mastering these advanced Groovy techniques, you can stay one step ahead in the ever-evolving world of cybersecurity.

## Writing Scripts to Monitor System Logs and Alerts

System logs provide vital insights into application behavior, user actions, and potential security issues. Additionally, setting up automated alerts for crucial log events can help system administrators respond promptly to incidents, thereby minimizing downtime and ensuring system reliability. In this chapter, we will explore how to use Groovy, a powerful scripting language that runs on the Java platform, to write scripts that monitor system logs and generate alerts based on predefined criteria.

## Understanding Groovy Basics

Before we dive into writing our log monitoring scripts, it's essential to understand some Groovy fundamentals. Groovy is an agile, dynamic language that integrates seamlessly with Java. Its syntax is similar to Java but provides features that make it easier and more expressive for scripting, such as:

**Dynamic Typing:** Variables do not need explicit type declarations.

**Closures:** Anonymous code blocks that can be executed at a later time.

**Built-in support for collections:** Easier manipulation of lists and maps. ### Setting Up the Environment

To write and run Groovy scripts, you will need:

**Java Development Kit (JDK):** Ensure that you have JDK installed on your machine.

**Groovy SDK:** Download and set up the Groovy SDK from the official website.

**Text Editor or IDE:** Use any text editor or IDE that supports Groovy development, such as IntelliJ IDEA or

Visual Studio Code.

## Reading System Logs

To monitor system logs, we'll begin by writing a simple Groovy script to read log files. For this purpose, we will utilize Groovy's built-in file handling capabilities, which allow us to read files line-by-line or even process them as streams.

### Sample Log File

Let's assume we have a log file named `system.log`, which contains entries like the following:

```
2023-10-25 14:32:00 INFO System started successfully

2023-10-25 14:33:12 WARN Disk space is below 20%
2023-10-25 14:34:00 ERROR Unable to connect to database

2023-10-25 14:35:00 INFO User logged in: user@example.com 2023-10-25 14:36:15 ERROR File not found: /path/to/file.txt
```

### Writing the Log Monitoring Script

We will write a Groovy script to monitor this log file and search for any lines containing the keywords "ERROR" or "WARN".

```groovy
def logFile = new File('system.log')
```

```
def alertKeywords = ['ERROR', 'WARN']

logFile.eachLine { line ->

if (alertKeywords.any { line.contains(it) }) { println "Alert: ${line}"

// Additional logic to send alert (email/SMS) can be added here.

}

}
```
```

### Explanation of the Script

**File Handling:** We create a `File` object pointing to `system.log`.

**Keywords Array:** We define an array of keywords that we want to monitor.

**Line Iteration:** The `eachLine` method iterates over each line in the log file.

**Condition Check:** The `any` method checks if any of the keywords appear in the current line. If a match is found, we print an alert message.

## Enhancing Functionality with Alerts

While logging alerts to the console is useful, in production systems, you will often want to implement an actual alerting mechanism (e.g., sending emails or notifications). For this, we can utilize the Java Mail API.

### Sending Email Alerts

To send email alerts, we will enhance our previous script.
```

Make sure you have the Java Mail API in your classpath.

```groovy
import javax.mail.*

import javax.mail.internet.*

def sendEmail(String subject, String body) { def properties
= new Properties()

properties.put("mail.smtp.host", "smtp.example.com") //
SMTP server properties.put("mail.smtp.port", "587")
properties.put("mail.smtp.auth", "true")


def session = Session.getInstance(properties, new
Authenticator() { @Override

protected                          PasswordAuthentication
getPasswordAuthentication()       {       return       new
PasswordAuthentication("username", "password")

}
})

try {

def     message     =     new     MimeMessage(session)
message.setFrom(new
InternetAddress("alert@example.com"))

message.setRecipients(Message.RecipientType.TO,
InternetAddress.parse("admin@example.com"))
message.setSubject(subject)

message.setText(body)
```

```
Transport.send(message)
println "Email alert sent successfully."
} catch (MessagingException e) { e.printStackTrace()
}
}

logFile.eachLine { line ->
if (alertKeywords.any { line.contains(it) }) { println "Alert: ${line}"
sendEmail("Log Alert", line)
}
}
```
` ` `

### Explanation of Email Alert Code

**Properties Setup:** Configuration properties for connecting to the SMTP server.

**Session Creation:** An authenticated email session is created.

**Message Creation:** A new email message is composed with the specified recipient, subject, and content.

**Sending the Email:** The `Transport.send` method sends the email, and we handle any potential exceptions.

In this chapter, we explored the basics of writing Groovy scripts for monitoring system logs and generating alerts based on specific keywords. We demonstrated how to read log files, identify critical events, and send email notifications for timely awareness of system issues. The flexibility and expressiveness of Groovy make it an excellent tool for system administration tasks, enabling automation and proactive monitoring.

# Building Intrusion Detection Automation with Groovy

Intrusion Detection Systems (IDS) have become essential components of network security. This chapter explores the development of an automated intrusion detection system using Groovy, a powerful and dynamic language that runs on the Java platform.

By leveraging Groovy's concise syntax and seamless integration with Java libraries, we can create a robust, flexible, and maintainable intrusion detection automation framework. This chapter will guide you through the essential steps necessary to build such a system, including setting up the environment, collecting and processing data, defining detection rules, and responding to detected intrusions.

## Setting Up the Environment

Before diving into the core development of the IDS, it's crucial to set up a suitable development environment. This includes installing Groovy and necessary libraries, as well as preparing the infrastructure for test data.

### Installing Groovy

**Download Groovy**: Visit the [Apache Groovy website](https://groovy.apache.org/download.html) and download the latest version.

**Install Groovy**: Follow the installation instructions for your operating system. For most Unix-based systems, you can use package managers like `sdkman` or directly set up the Groovy environment using binaries.

### Setting Up a Development IDE

While Groovy code can be written in any text editor, using an Integrated Development Environment (IDE) enhances efficiency. Popular choices include:

IntelliJ IDEA with Groovy plugin

Eclipse with Groovy Development Tools (GSDE)

Visual Studio Code with Groovy support ### Library Dependencies

For this project, we'll utilize a few libraries that enhance Groovy's capabilities:

**Apache Commons Lang**: For utility functions.

**Log4j**: For logging events and alerts.

**Spring Framework**: For handling configuration and dependency injection.

You can define these dependencies in a build tool like Gradle or Maven to manage them efficiently. ## Collecting and Processing Data

An IDS requires real-time data collection from the network to effectively analyze and detect potential intrusions. This section provides an overview of methods for collecting network data and the structure for processing it.

### Data Sources

**Network Traffic Monitoring**: Capturing packets using tools like Wireshark or tcpdump.

**System Logs**: Analyzing logs from servers, firewalls, and applications to identify suspicious activity. ### Implementing Data Collection

Using Groovy's capabilities, we can create classes to handle data collection. Here's a simple implementation of a packet listener:

```groovy
@Grab(group='org.pcap4j', module='pcap4j-core', version='1.8.0') import org.pcap4j.core.*

import org.pcap4j.core.PcapNetworkInterface

import org.pcap4j.core.PcapNetworkInterface.PromiscuousMode

class PacketListener { PcapNetworkInterface networkInterface

PacketListener(String interfaceName) {

networkInterface = Pcaps.findDeviceByName(interfaceName) if (networkInterface == null) {

throw new IllegalArgumentException("Network interface not found: $interfaceName")

}

}

void startListening() throws PcapNativeException {

networkInterface.openLive(65536, PromiscuousMode.PROMISCUOUS, 10,
```

```groovy
null).packetDump(packet -
> {
// Process packet (conversion to string representation,
etc.) println "Packet captured: ${packet}"
// Further processing...
})
}
}
```

In this code snippet, we create a `PacketListener` class
that will open a network interface for live packet
capturing.

## Defining Detection Rules

Once data is collected, you need to define rules for what
constitutes an intrusion. Rules can be defined using
Groovy's powerful programming constructs.

### Rule Structure

Here's a simple example of how you might define rules for
detecting suspicious activity, such as repeated failed login
attempts:

```groovy
class IntrusionRule { String name

Closure<Boolean> condition

IntrusionRule(String name, Closure<Boolean> condition)
{ this.name = name

this.condition = condition
```

```groovy
}
boolean     evaluate(Event     event)     {     return
condition.call(event)
}
}
// Example usage
def rule = new IntrusionRule("Multiple Failed Logins") {
event -> event.failedLoginCount > 5
}
```

In this example, the `IntrusionRule` class takes a name and a condition as input. The condition is a closure (anonymous function) evaluated against incoming events to determine if an intrusion is occurring.

## Responding to Detected Intrusions

Automating the response to intrusions is critical for an effective IDS. Depending on the severity of the intrusion, responses may vary from alerts to blocking IP addresses.

### Implementing Response Mechanisms

You could implement a simple alert system using the following structure:

```groovy
class AlertSystem {
void sendAlert(String message) { println "ALERT: $message"
// Additional alert mechanisms (email, SMS, etc.)
```

167

```
}
void blockIP(String ipAddress) { println "Blocking IP:
$ipAddress"

// Logic to block IP (firewall commands, etc.)

}
}

// Example of usage in connection with rules def
alertSystem = new AlertSystem()

if              (rule.evaluate(event))              {
alertSystem.sendAlert("Intrusion detected: ${event}")
alertSystem.blockIP(event.sourceIP)

}
```
` ` `

With the `AlertSystem` class, we can send alerts and take action such as blocking an IP address in response to detected intrusions.

Building an automated Intrusion Detection System using Groovy allows for the integration of dynamic detection capabilities and flexible response mechanisms. As we have explored in this chapter, Groovy's

simplicity and power make it an excellent choice for creating security applications.

# Conclusion

Congratulations on making it to the end of *"Groovy*

*Programming Language for DevSecOps: Agile Scripting to Secure and Streamline Software Delivery With Groovy!"* 🎉 Throughout this book, we've explored how Groovy isn't just another programming language—it's a game-changer for integrating security, agility, and automation into your software delivery pipelines.

From writing security scripts that catch vulnerabilities early to automating audits that save you time (and headaches), Groovy has proven to be a versatile ally in tackling modern DevSecOps challenges. We've dived into the practical side of using Groovy to:

**Create custom security scripts** that adapt to your team's needs.

**Perform automated audits** to ensure compliance and best practices.

**Seamlessly integrate DevSecOps practices** into CI/CD pipelines.

The power of Groovy lies not just in its syntax or libraries but in its ability to simplify complex workflows and empower developers, security experts, and operations teams to collaborate more effectively. With Groovy, you can break down silos, enhance security, and deliver software that's not only fast but also reliable and safe.

But remember, DevSecOps isn't a one-time task—it's a mindset. The tools and techniques you've learned here are just the beginning. Keep experimenting, keep automating, and most importantly, keep prioritizing security as a core part of your development process.

Now it's your turn to take the concepts, scripts, and strategies you've learned and make them your own.

Whether you're securing an application, optimizing a pipeline, or mentoring your team on Groovy best practices, you have the tools to make a meaningful impact.

Thank you for joining me on this journey. Here's to building faster, safer, and more secure software—one Groovy script at a time. Happy coding, and may your pipelines always run green!

# Biography

**Davis Simon** is a passionate software developer, seasoned backend architect, and advocate for clean, efficient code. With over a decade of experience in web application development, Davis has built scalable, high-performing systems for startups and enterprises alike. His expertise lies in backend development and leveraging the power of languages like Groovy to create APIs and microservices that are as robust as they are elegant.

A self-proclaimed "Groovy enthusiast," Davis discovered the language early in his career and quickly fell in love with its versatility and simplicity. His dedication to Groovy programming inspired him to write this book and share his insights with aspiring developers looking to harness its potential for backend development.

When he's not writing code or crafting the next big web application, Davis enjoys exploring emerging technologies, mentoring new developers, and experimenting with creative ways to solve programming challenges. Outside of the tech world, Davis is an avid gamer and a lover of all things sci-fi, often finding inspiration for his projects in futuristic tales and virtual worlds.

With this eBook, Davis invites you to join him on a journey to revolutionize backend development with Groovy. His approachable teaching style and practical advice will empower you to take your skills to the next level—whether you're building your first API or architecting complex systems.

# Glossary: Groovy Programming Language for DevSecOps

## Key Terminology ### 1. **Groovy**

An agile and dynamic language for the Java Virtual Machine (JVM), Groovy is designed to simplify Java development. It incorporates features from other programming languages while maintaining compatibility with Java, making it easier to write concise and expressive code.

### 2. **DevSecOps**

A cultural and technical movement that integrates security practices within the DevOps process. By ensuring that security is a shared responsibility involving all participants in the software development lifecycle, it aims to enhance security posture without sacrificing speed or efficiency.

### 3. **Continuous Integration/Continuous Deployment (CI/CD)**

A set of practices and tools that automate the integration of code changes from multiple contributors into a shared repository and deploy applications as code changes are made. Groovy is often used in CI/CD pipelines, especially with tools like Jenkins.

### 4. **Jenkins**

An open-source automation server widely used for CI/CD. It allows developers to automate building, testing, and deploying applications. Groovy is commonly used in Jenkins for scripting and configuring the deployment pipelines.

### 5. **Pipeline**

A series of automated processes defined in code that facilitate the progress of software development, from code commit to deployment. In the context of Groovy and Jenkins, pipelines are often written using Groovy syntax to define steps, execution scripts, and stages.

### 6. **Scripted Pipeline**

A type of Jenkins pipeline that is defined using Groovy scripts, enabling the flexibility and versatility essential for advanced configurations and control over the execution flow.

### 7. **Declarative Pipeline**

A simpler and more structured alternative to the scripted pipeline format in Jenkins. It provides a more straightforward syntax to define the pipeline stages, allowing developers to focus more on the "what" instead of the "how."

### 8. **Groovy DSL (Domain-specific Language)**

Groovy supports the creation of DSLs that provide a tailored language for specific problem domains. For instance, Jenkins Pipelines can be viewed as a DSL for defining the lifecycle of DevSecOps processes.

### 9. **Static Code Analysis**

The process of analyzing source code without executing it, often used to identify potential security vulnerabilities and compliance issues. Groovy supports various static analysis tools, allowing DevSecOps teams to integrate security checks into their development pipelines.

### 10. **Testing Framework**

Groovy has built-in support for testing through frameworks like Spock and Geb, which facilitate behavior-

driven development (BDD) and browser testing. These frameworks ensure that security features are well- tested within the continuous integration pipeline.

### 11. **Dependency Management**

In Groovy, dependency management tools like Grape and Gradle help manage libraries and dependencies for projects. Proper management of dependencies is critical in the DevSecOps model for ensuring that third- party libraries do not introduce vulnerabilities.

### 12. **Infrastructure as Code (IaC)**

Managing infrastructure through code rather than manual processes. Groovy can be used within IaC tools like Terraform and Ansible for automating the provisioning and management of infrastructure, including security controls.

### 13. **Vulnerability Scanning**

The automated process of identifying security weaknesses

within applications or their configurations. Integrating Groovy scripts within CI/CD pipelines can help automate vulnerability scanning, alerting developers of potential issues early.

### 14. **Containerization**

The packaging of applications and their dependencies into containers, which can run consistently across various computing environments. Groovy can facilitate the automation of container management through tools like Docker and Kubernetes, helping maintain secure configurations.

### 15. **Secrets Management**

The practice of securely storing and accessing credentials, API keys, and sensitive information. Utilizing Groovy in conjunction with secrets management tools can ensure that such sensitive data is handled securely in DevSecOps pipelines.

### 16. **Version Control**

The system that records changes to code over time. Utilizing version control systems like Git is essential in DevSecOps practices, allowing teams to track changes, collaborate, and manage release versions effectively. Groovy scripts can be integrated to enhance version control processes.

### 17. **Security as Code**

The integration of security practices into the development process through automated checks and controls defined in code. Groovy facilitates the implementation of security as code by allowing developers to write comprehensive security tests as part of their CI/CD pipelines.

### 18. **Configuration Management**

The process of maintaining computer systems, servers, and software in a desired, consistent state. Tools utilizing Groovy can aid in automating configuration management within DevSecOps, ensuring seamless deployments while minimizing security risks.

### 19. **Policy as Code**

A practice in which governance and compliance policies are defined in a machine-readable format. Groovy can be utilized to enforce policies in automated deployments, ensuring that compliance and security are inherently integrated into the development lifecycle.

### 20. **Feedback Loops**

The process of gathering continuous feedback from different stages of development and deployment. In a DevSecOps context, Groovy scripts can be implemented to create automated feedback mechanisms that identify security issues immediately after code changes are made.


### Introduction

In today's fast-paced digital landscape, the convergence of development, security, and operations—collectively known as DevSecOps—has become essential for organizations striving to streamline their software delivery pipelines while ensuring robust security practices. As businesses increasingly rely on rapid software development and deployment, the need for effective automation and integration of security into the DevOps lifecycle has never been more critical.

This is where the Groovy programming language comes into play. Recognized for its simplicity, dynamic nature, and seamless compatibility with the Java platform, Groovy stands out as a powerful tool for scripting within DevSecOps environments. Its expressive syntax and flexibility allow developers and operations teams to craft scripts that automate workflows, integrate security measures, and enhance the overall efficiency of the software delivery process.

In "Groovy Programming Language for DevSecOps: Agile Scripting to Secure and Streamline Software Delivery With Groovy," we delve into the myriad ways Groovy can support you in achieving your DevSecOps objectives. This ebook is structured to guide you through the intricacies of the Groovy language while emphasizing its applications in securing applications and automating workflows. Whether you are a seasoned developer, a DevOps practitioner, or a security professional, this book is designed to empower you with the knowledge and skills to leverage Groovy effectively.

You'll start by understanding the core principles of Groovy, including its syntax, features, and best practices. From there, we will explore how to leverage Groovy for automating CI/CD pipelines, integrating security testing, and orchestrating infrastructure as code (IaC) workflows. Each chapter is filled with practical examples, code snippets, and real-world scenarios to illustrate how Groovy can simplify complex tasks, reduce manual overhead, and strengthen your security posture.

By the end of this journey, you will not only have a comprehensive understanding of Groovy but also the confidence to implement its capabilities in your

DevSecOps practices. Join us as we explore the synergy between Groovy and DevSecOps, paving the way for secure, efficient, and agile software delivery in an ever-evolving technological environment. Welcome to a new era of programming and security—welcome to Groovy.